National 5
CHEMISTRY

For SQA 2019 and beyond

Revision + Practice
2 Books in 1

© 2020 Leckie

001/01102020

10 9 8 7 6 5 4 3 2 1

ISBN 9780008435356

Published by
Leckie
An imprint of HarperCollinsPublishers
Westerhill Road, Bishopbriggs, Glasgow, G64 2QT
T: 0844 576 8126
leckiescotland@harpercollins.co.uk   www.leckiescotland.co.uk

Publisher: Sarah Mitchell
Project Manager: Harley Griffiths and Lauren Murray

Special thanks to
QBS (layout and illustration)

Printed in Italy by Grafica Veneta S.p.A

A CIP Catalogue record for this book is available from the British Library.

Acknowledgements
We would like to thank the following for permission to reproduce their material:
p. 26 POWER AND SYRED/SCIENCE PHOTO LIBRARY; p. 73 ANDREWLAMBERT PHOTOGRAPHY/SCIENCE PHOTO LIBRARY; p. 74 E. R. DEGGINGER/SCIENCE PHOTO LIBRARY; p. 94 MARTYN F. CHILLMAID/SCIENCE PHOTO LIBRARY

All other images © Shutterstock.com

ebook

To access the ebook version of this Revision Guide visit
www.collins.co.uk/ebooks
and follow the step-by-step instructions.

Contents

Contents

Area 2: Nature's chemistry

Area 3: Chemistry in society

Glossary   101

Part 2: Practice exam papers

ANSWERS *Check your answers to the practice test papers online:*
www.leckieandleckie.co.uk

Introduction

Complete Revision and Practice

This Complete **two-in-one Revision and Practice book** is designed to support you as students of National 5 Chemistry. It can be used either in the classroom, for regular study and homework, or for exam revision. By combining **a revision guide and two full sets of practice exam papers**, this book includes everything you need to be fully familiar with the National 5 Chemistry exam. As well as including ALL the core course content with practice opportunities, there is comprehensive assignment and exam preparation advice included. This book has also been designed for easy reference with a glossary at the end of the revision guide, and both revision question and practice test paper answers provided online at www.leckieandleckie.co.uk.

LECKIE
the education publisher
for Scotland

National 5
CHEMISTRY

For SQA 2019 and beyond

Revision Guide

Bob Wilson

Rates of reaction 1

Monitoring the rate of reaction

The rate of chemical reactions can be monitored in a number of ways. A simple way is to measure the **volume of gas** produced in a reaction over time, then draw a graph of the results. The **loss in mass** over time can also be used to monitor the progress of a reaction. A suitable reaction is marble chips (pieces of calcium carbonate) reacting with hydrochloric acid. Carbon dioxide gas is produced.

The arrangements which can be used are shown on pages 12 and 14.

Graph 1 shows how the volume of gas produced in a reaction between calcium carbonate and hydrochloric acid changes with time.

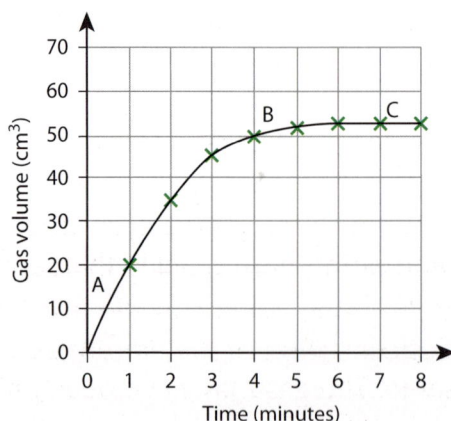

Graph 1

- At A, near the start of the reaction: the line is almost a straight line with a fairly steep slope. The gas is being produced quickly. The reaction is **fast**.
- At B, towards the end of the reaction: the line starts to level off. The gas is not being produced as quickly. The reaction is **slowing down**.
- At C, at the end of the reaction: the line has completely levelled off. All of the marble has reacted. No more gas is being produced. The reaction has **stopped**. This is the end-point of the reaction.

Increasing the concentration

The effect on the rate of reaction of repeating the experiment with more concentrated acid is shown in graph 2.

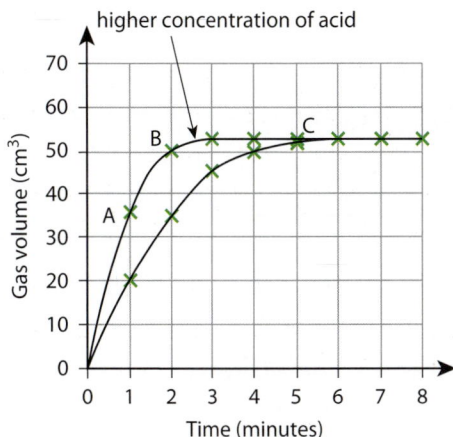

Graph 2

- At A, the line has a much steeper slope than with the lower concentration of acid. The reaction is much **faster**.
- At B, the line starts to level off more quickly than in the first experiment. The reaction is nearing the end-point more quickly than at the lower concentration.
- At C, the end-point is at the same volume as the first experiment. This is because, although the concentration of the acid has changed, the mass of marble reacting is the same. The gas may have been produced more quickly at the higher concentration but the same final volume of gas is produced in both experiments.

Increasing the temperature

If the experiment is carried out at two different temperatures and the loss in mass as the gas is produced is measured, graph 3 is produced.

- At A, there is a much steeper slope at the higher temperature. The reaction is much **faster** at the higher temperature.
- At B, the line at the higher temperature starts to level off more quickly than at the lower temperature. The reaction is nearing the end point more quickly than at the lower temperature.
- At C, the end-point is at the same volume as the first experiment. This is because, although the temperature of the acid has changed, the mass of marble reacting is the same. The reaction may happen more quickly at the higher temperature but the same final volume of gas is produced in both experiments.

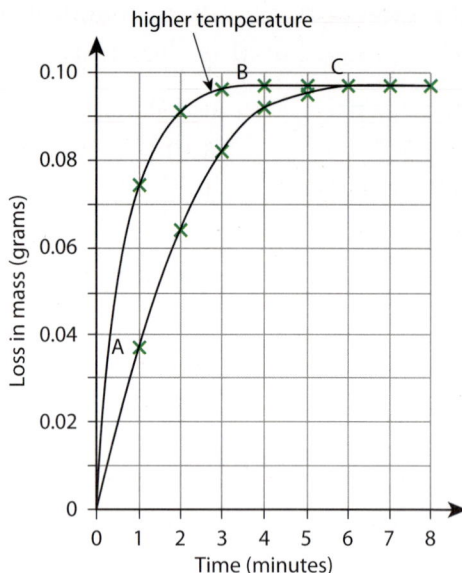

Graph 3

Decreasing the particle size

The effect on the rate of reaction of repeating the experiment with different sizes of marble chips is shown in graph 4.

The shape of each line can be explained as with the previous graphs. The slope of the line with the powdered marble is much steeper than with lumps of marble. indicating that the reaction was **faster** when the marble is **powdered** as it has a larger surface area for the acid to react with.

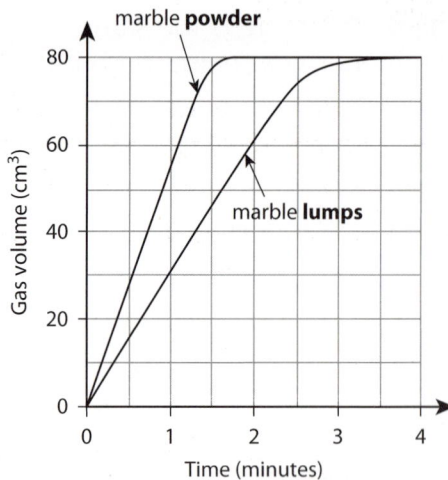

Graph 4

Measuring total loss in mass of flask and contents

Sometimes the change in the total mass of the reaction flask and its contents over time is measured and a graph plotted. Graph 5 shows the type of curve obtained.

Although the shape of the graph is different to the other graphs in this section it can be interpreted in the same way.

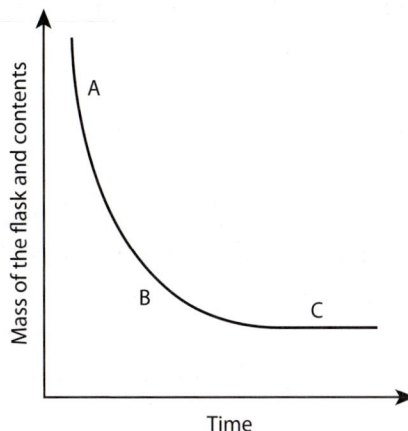

Graph 5

- At A, the graph is a steep straight line showing that the reaction is fast. The reactants are being used up quickly.
- At B, the graph is less steep showing the reaction is slowing down because the reactants are being used up.
- At C, the graph has levelled off. At least one of the reactants is completely used up and the reaction has stopped. This is the end point of the reaction.

Quick Test

1. Powdered zinc metal can be reacted completely with hydrochloric acid. One of the products is hydrogen gas. The volume of hydrogen produced can be measured and the results used to see how the rate of reaction changes over time.

    (a) Describe how you could carry out an experiment to measure the volume of gas produced over time.

    (b) The rate-of-reaction graph produced from the results of an experiment like the one you described in part (a) is shown.

    (i) How do the rates of reaction at points A, B and C on the graph compare?

    (ii) Explain how the shape of the line at points A, B and C helped you to answer part (b) (i).

    (c) What volume of hydrogen gas was produced at the end point?

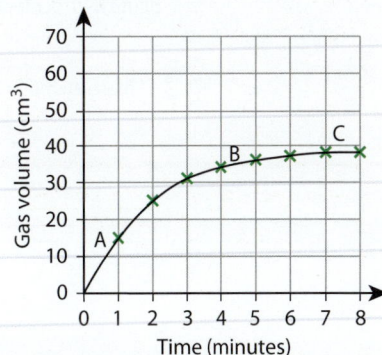

    (d) (i) Sketch the graph above and add another graph to show what happens when the reaction is carried out with a higher concentration of acid.

    (You do not need to use graph paper or include the scales on the graph.)

    (ii) Explain the shape of this graph compared to the original.

Rates of reaction 2

Speeding up chemical reactions

The rate of a reaction can be increased by: increasing the concentration of reactants; decreasing the particle size; raising the temperature and adding a catalyst.

A catalyst is a substance which can speed up a chemical reaction and can be recovered unchanged at the end of the reaction.

Calculating average rate of reaction

The **average rate** of a chemical reaction is the change in the quantity of reactant or product over time and can be calculated using data collected from experiments carried out in the laboratory.

A suitable reaction is marble chips (containing calcium carbonate) reacting with hydrochloric acid:

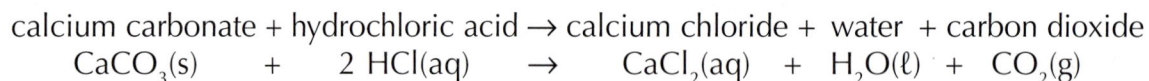

calcium carbonate + hydrochloric acid → calcium chloride + water + carbon dioxide

$$CaCO_3(s) \quad + \quad 2\,HCl(aq) \quad \rightarrow \quad CaCl_2(aq) \quad + \quad H_2O(\ell) \quad + \quad CO_2(g)$$

Measuring the change in volume of gas produced during the reaction

The rate at which carbon dioxide gas is given off can be measured by collecting the gas and measuring the volume at fixed time intervals. Collecting the gas by displacement of water is the most commonly used method in the laboratory, but using a syringe gives more accurate measurements.

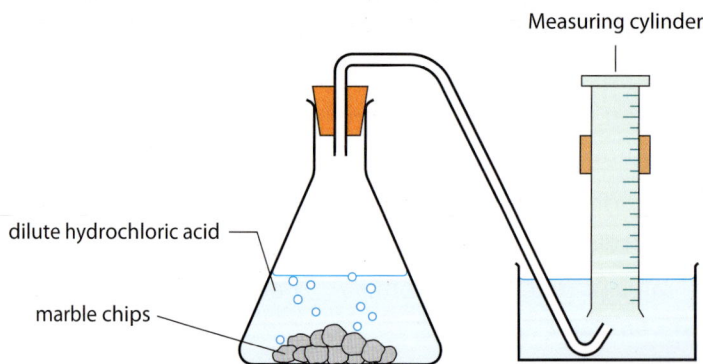

Measuring cylinder

dilute hydrochloric acid

marble chips

The graph shows how the volume of gas changes over the course of the reaction.

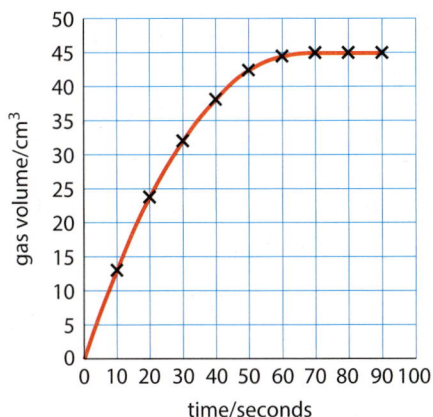

Graph of volume of gas produced over time.

Remember!

$$\text{Average rate} = \frac{\text{change in volume}}{\text{change in time}}$$

The information required is obtained from the graph.

Example 1

Calculate the average rate of reaction over the first 10 seconds.

Worked answer:

$$\text{Average rate of reaction} = \frac{\text{volume at 10 s – volume at 0 s}}{\text{time interval}} = \frac{13 - 0}{10 - 0} = \textbf{1.3 cm}^3 \textbf{ s}^{-1}$$

Since rate here is a measure of the change in volume of the gas over time, the unit of rate is **cm³ s⁻¹** (cubic centimetres per second).

Measuring the loss in mass during a reaction

The rate at which carbon dioxide is given off is obtained by measuring the loss in mass of the reactants at regular time intervals. As the gas is produced, it is released into the air so the mass of the reaction mixture and flask decreases.

The graph shows how the mass changes over the course of the reaction.

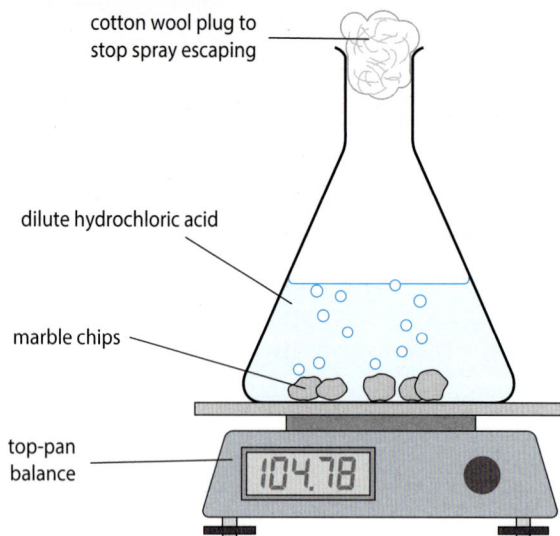

cotton wool plug to stop spray escaping

dilute hydrochloric acid

marble chips

top-pan balance

104.78

Remember!

$$\text{Average rate} = \frac{\text{change in mass}}{\text{change in time}}$$

The information required is obtained from the graph.

Example 2

Calculate the average rate of reaction between 20 and 40 seconds.

Worked answer:

$$\text{Average rate of reaction} = \frac{\text{mass loss at 40 s} - \text{mass loss at 20 s}}{\text{time interval}} = \frac{0.38 - 0.24}{40 - 20}$$

Average rate of reaction = 0.007 g s^{-1}

Since rate here is a measure of the mass loss over time, the unit of rate is **g s^{-1}** (grams per second).

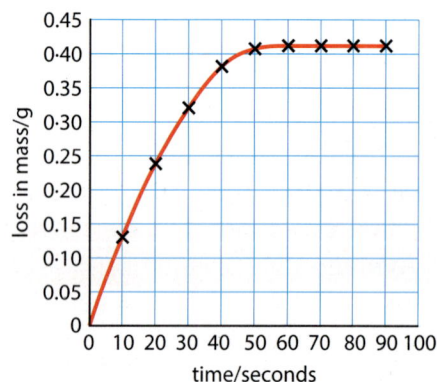

Graph of loss of mass over time.

(y-axis: loss in mass/g, values 0, 0.05, 0.10, 0.15, 0.20, 0.25, 0.30, 0.35, 0.40, 0.45; x-axis: time/seconds, values 0 to 100)

TOP TIP

The relationship between rate and change in (Δ) quantity with time (t) is given in the SQA data booklet as

$$\text{rate} = \frac{\Delta \text{ quantity}}{\Delta t}$$

Quick Test

1. Look at the graph of volume of gas against time. Calculate the average rate of reaction between 30 and 50 seconds.

2. Look at the graph of loss of mass against time. Calculate the average rate of reaction over the first 20 seconds.

Atoms and the periodic table

Atoms

All substances are made up of **atoms**. Atoms contain particles called **protons (p)**, **neutrons (n)** and **electrons (e⁻)**. The diagrams shows how these particles are arranged in atoms.

The left-hand diagram gives the idea that atoms are not flat and electrons are moving. The right-hand diagram is known as a 'target diagram' and shows the electrons arranged in shells, like the layers in an onion.

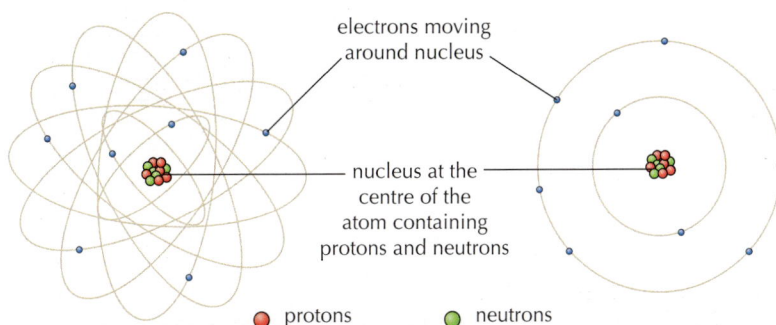

electrons moving around nucleus

nucleus at the centre of the atom containing protons and neutrons

protons   neutrons

Each particle has a charge and mass, as shown in the table.

Particle	Charge	Mass
proton (p)	one positive (+)	1
electron (e⁻)	one negative (–)	almost zero
neutron (n)	no charge (0)	1

The number of protons in an atom identifies which element the atom belongs to. The number of protons is known as the **atomic number**. In an atom the number of protons is the same as the number of electrons. The positive charge of the protons is balanced by the negative charge of the electrons so, overall, an atom is neutral (neutrons have no charge).

If the atomic number is known the element can be identified and the number of protons and electrons in each atom can be worked out.

Example 1

An element has an atomic number of 3. Using the Periodic Table, the element can be identified as lithium. Each lithium atom must have 3 protons and 3 electrons.

Example 2

Chlorine has an atomic number of 17, so a chlorine atom has 17 protons and 17 electrons.

Example 3

An atom has 10 protons. Its atomic number must be 10 and so the element is neon.

The mass of an atom is due to the mass of the protons and neutrons. The mass of the protons added to the mass of the neutrons is known as the **mass number**. The electrons are so light that they don't affect the mass.

mass number = number of protons + number of neutrons

The number of neutrons can be calculated by subtracting the atomic number from the mass number.

number of neutrons = mass number − atomic number

Example 4

An atom of sodium has 12 neutrons. Calculate its mass number.

From the Periodic Table, the atomic number of sodium is 11. The atom must have 11 protons.

mass number = number of protons + number of neutrons

= 11 + 12

mass number = 23

Periodic table

Elements are substances made from the same atoms. The Periodic Table shows elements with similar chemical properties arranged in families. Elements in the same vertical **group** have the same **valency** and react in a similar way – they have similar chemical properties. Each element has its own symbol and atomic number. Metals are found on the left of the periodic table and non-metals to the right.

The electrons in an atom are arranged in an organised way. The electrons move around the nucleus in layers of space, sometimes called shells, a bit like the layers in an onion. This can be shown in a target diagram.

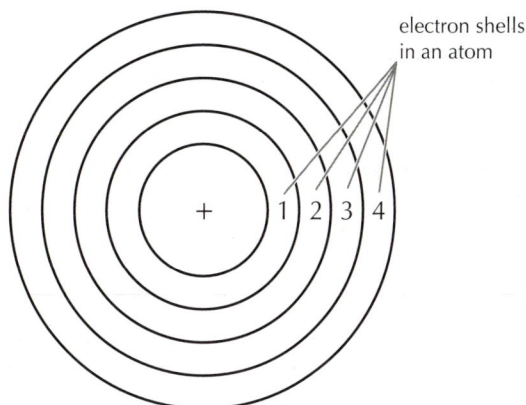

electron shells in an atom

The number of electrons in the outer shell of an atom is the same as the group number of the element in the periodic table. The electron arrangement for the elements are written in a way which shows how many electrons are in each shell.

Electron shells in an atom

Example 1: Potassium (atomic number 19), in group 1: 2,8,8,1

Example 2: Chlorine (atomic number 17), in group 1: 2,8,7

TOP TIP

You only need to be able to write the electron arrangement of the first 20 elements. They are found in the SQA data booklet.

Quick Test

1   The table gives information about the atoms of two elements. Use a periodic table to help you complete entries (a) – (j).

Element	Symbol	Atomic number	Protons	Electrons	Neutrons	Mass number
carbon	(a)	(b)	(c)	(d)	8	(e)
(f)	(g)	(h)	17	(i)	(j)	35

2   a Write the electron arrangement for

   i aluminium   ii sulfur

   b Draw a target diagram showing the arrangement of the electrons in an atom of boron.

   c State the relationship between the number of outer electrons in an atom of an element and the position of the element in the periodic table.

Nuclide notation, isotopes and relative atomic mass (RAM)

Nuclide notation

Nuclide notation is a shorthand way of showing the mass number and atomic number of an **atom** along with the symbol of the element. The nuclide notation for an atom of chlorine, atomic number 17, with a mass number of 35, can be used as an example:

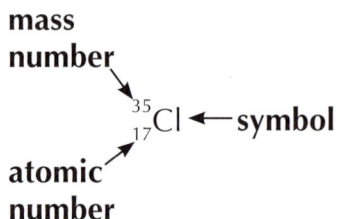

$$\text{mass number} \searrow \quad \atom{^{35}_{17}Cl} \leftarrow \text{symbol} \quad \text{atomic number} \nearrow$$

Nuclide notation can also be used for **ions**. The number of electrons (e⁻) is the only thing that changes when an atom forms an ion. This means the atomic number and the mass number do not change. The nuclide notation for an atom and ion of chlorine is shown below.

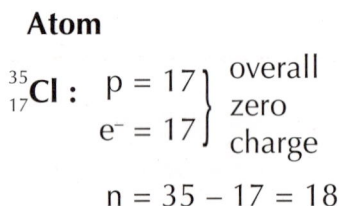

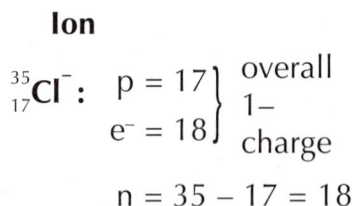

Atom

$^{35}_{17}Cl :$ $\left.\begin{array}{l} p = 17 \\ e^- = 17 \end{array}\right\}$ overall zero charge

$n = 35 - 17 = 18$

Ion

$^{35}_{17}Cl^- :$ $\left.\begin{array}{l} p = 17 \\ e^- = 18 \end{array}\right\}$ overall 1− charge

$n = 35 - 17 = 18$

Isotopes

Atoms that have the same atomic number but different mass numbers are known as **isotopes**. Some atoms of chlorine, for example, have 18 neutrons, while others have 20 neutrons. This means their mass numbers are different (35 and 37) but their atomic numbers are the same (17). The nuclide notation for the two isotopes of chlorine is: $^{35}_{17}Cl$ and $^{37}_{17}Cl$.

Remember!
The isotopes of an element have the same electron arrangement so they have identical chemical behaviour.

Relative Atomic Mass (RAM)

The total mass of an atom comes from the mass of its neutrons and protons. Most elements however have two or more isotopes so an average is taken of the mass of all the isotopes. This average mass is called the **relative atomic mass (RAM).**

We get the information needed to calculate the relative atomic mass from a mass spectrometer. The information is often given in a graph.

From the graph we can see that:

* Chlorine has two isotopes – corresponding to the two peaks.
* The isotopes have atoms of mass 35 and 37.
* 75% of atoms have a mass of 35, and 25% have a mass of 37.

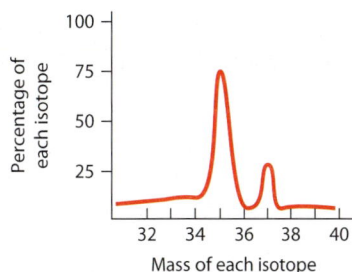

The graph shows the percentage of the two isotopes of chlorine.

This information can be used to calculate the relative atomic mass of chlorine:

$$\text{RAM} = \frac{(75 \times 35) + (25 \times 37)}{100} = \textbf{35.5}$$

Quick Test

1. An atom of bromine has 44 neutrons and 35 protons.

    (a) Write the nuclide notation for the atom.

    (b) When the atom forms an ion, it gains an electron. Write the nuclide notation for the bromide ion.

    (c) Bromine has two stable isotopes, $^{79}_{35}\text{Br}$ and $^{81}_{35}\text{Br}$. The relative atomic mass of bromine is sometimes rounded up to 80. What can you deduce about the percentage abundance of each isotope?

2. The table gives information about the three naturally occurring isotopes of neon.

Isotope	Percentage abundance
^{20}Ne	90.5
^{21}Ne	0.3
^{22}Ne	9.2

Calculate the relative atomic mass of neon.

Covalent bonding and shapes of molecules

Single covalent bonds

Atoms of non-metal elements achieve the stable electron arrangement of the noble gases by sharing outer electrons and forming a covalent bond.

The two fluorine atoms in a fluorine molecule are held together by a **single** covalent bond – a **shared pair of electrons**. This can be shown in a dot and cross diagram.

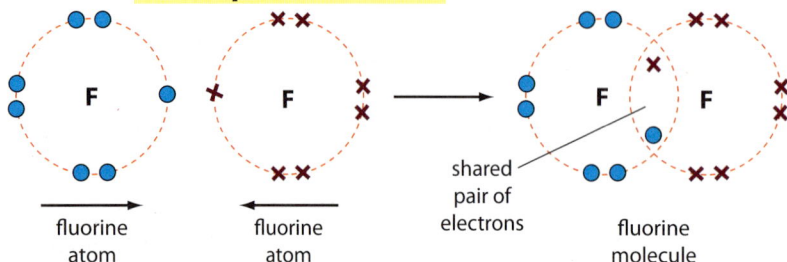

Two fluorine atoms forming a fluorine molecule.

In a covalent bond, the positive nucleus of each atom attracts not only its own electrons but also the electrons from the other atom.

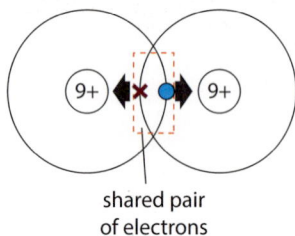

The nucleus of one atom attracts the electrons of the other.

Count the electrons in the outer energy level of each atom in the fluorine molecule – each has seven electrons of its own and a share in an eighth. Eight electrons is a stable arrangement.

A hydrogen atom and a chlorine atom join to form a hydrogen chloride molecule – only the outer electrons are shown for the chlorine atom:

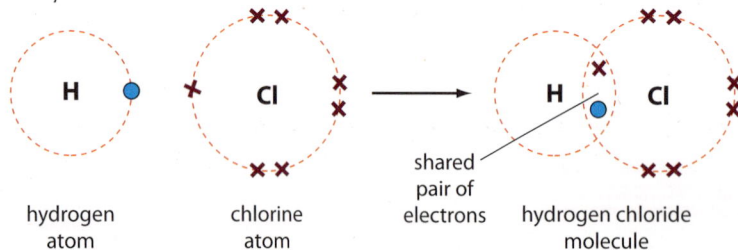

This dot and cross diagram shows a hydrogen atom and a chlorine atom joining.

Count the number of electrons in the outer energy level of each atom in the molecule. Chlorine has eight electrons, the stable arrangement. Hydrogen has two electrons, which at first glance is not a stable arrangement, but it is the same arrangement as the noble gas helium – two electrons in the first (only) energy level is a stable arrangement.

Fluorine and hydrogen chloride are **diatomic molecules** – fluorine is an element and hydrogen chloride a compound. They have a **linear** shape – their atoms are in a line. A fluorine molecule can be written as F–F and hydrogen chloride as H–Cl. This representation shows both the covalent bond and the shape of the molecule.

Hydrogen, H_2

Sharing their electron gives each hydrogen atom a filled outer energy level. The hydrogen molecule is diatomic.

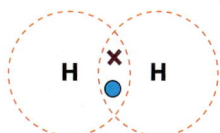

This can also be shown as **H — H**

Two hydrogen atoms joining.

TOP TIP

The diatomic elements are hydrogen, oxygen, nitrogen and the halogens.

The shape of a hydrogen molecule is **linear**.

Water, H_2O

Atoms of oxygen and hydrogen combine by sharing pairs of electrons to form water. The oxygen atom has six outer electrons so needs two more. Oxygen forms two single covalent bonds to hydrogen atoms:

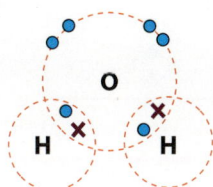

This can also be shown as

Oxygen and hydrogen sharing electrons.

The shape of a water molecule is **angular.**

Ammonia, NH_3

Atoms of nitrogen and hydrogen combine by sharing pairs of electrons to form ammonia. The nitrogen atom has five outer electrons so needs three more. Nitrogen forms three single covalent bonds to hydrogen atoms:

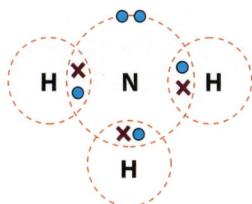

This can also be shown as

Nitrogen and hydrogen sharing electrons.

The shape of an ammonia molecule is **trigonal pyramidal**.

Methane, CH$_4$

Atoms of carbon and hydrogen combine by sharing pairs of electrons to form methane. The carbon atom has four outer electrons so needs four more. Carbon forms four single covalent bonds to hydrogen atoms:

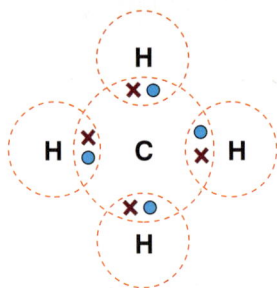

This can also be shown as

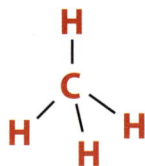

Carbon and hydrogen sharing electrons.

> **TOP TIP**
> The table gives a general rule about the number of atoms in a molecule with single bonds and the shape of the molecule.

The shape of a methane molecule is **tetrahedral**.

Number of atoms in molecule	Shape of molecule
two	linear
three	angular
four	trigonal pyramidal
five	tetrahedral

Numbers of atoms and the shapes of molecules.

Double and triple covalent bonds

It is possible for the atoms of non-metal elements to join together in such a way as to form **double** and even **triple** covalent bonds.

Oxygen, O$_2$

Both oxygen atoms have six outer electrons so both need two more electrons to form a stable arrangement of electrons (eight). They do this by sharing two pairs of electrons forming a double covalent bond:

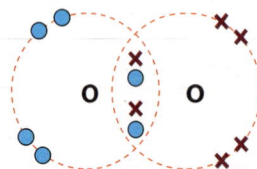

This can also be shown as **O = O**

Electrons being shared by two oxygen atoms.

Nitrogen, N_2

Both nitrogen atoms have five outer electrons so both need three more electrons to form a stable arrangement of electrons. They do this by sharing three pairs of electrons forming a triple covalent bond:

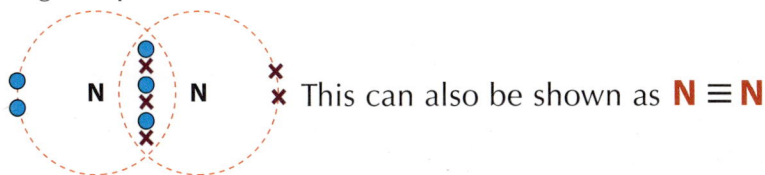

This can also be shown as $N \equiv N$

Two nitrogen atoms joining.

Carbon dioxide, CO_2

Carbon has four outer electrons so needs four more. It forms double covalent bonds with two oxygen atoms so that all the atoms now have a full outer shell of electrons:

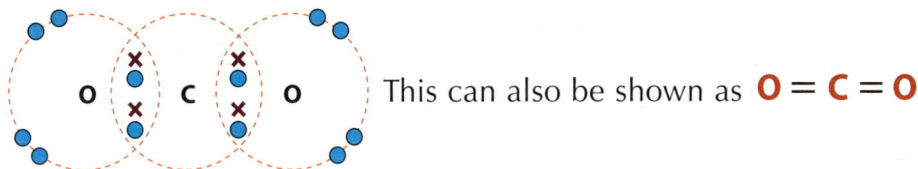

This can also be shown as $O = C = O$

Formation of carbon dioxide.

Note that the shape of the carbon dioxide molecule is linear and not bent as might be expected, because of the double bonds.

Quick Test

1. Hydrogen selenide is a flammable gas formed between hydrogen and selenium.

   (a) Draw a dot and cross diagram to show how hydrogen and selenium atoms join to form a molecule.

   (b) Draw the likely shape of hydrogen selenide.

   (c) Write the molecular formula for hydrogen selenide.

2. (a) Draw a dot and cross diagram to show how phosphorus and hydrogen atoms join to form a molecule.

   (b) Draw the likely shape of the molecule formed in (a).

   (c) Write the molecular formula for the compound.

3. Silane is formed when hydrogen reacts with silicon.

   (a) Draw a dot and cross diagram to show how hydrogen and silicon atoms join to form a molecule.

   (b) Draw the likely shape of silane.

   (c) Write the molecular formula for silane.

4. (a) Use dot and cross diagrams to show how carbon and sulfur atoms join to form carbon disulfide (CS_2).

   (b) Draw the likely shape of the carbon disulfide molecule.

(Hint: look at how carbon dioxide is formed.)

Structure and properties of covalent substances

Covalent molecular

Covalent substances that are made up of individual <mark>molecules</mark> can exist as gases, liquids or solids at room temperature.

The table shows the melting and boiling points of some covalent molecular substances and their states at room temperature. Note how the melting and boiling points increase as you move across from gases to liquids to solids.

gases	liquids	solids
$O=O$ O_2: mp = −218 °C bp = −183 °C	Br — Br Br_2: mp = −7 °C bp = 59 °C	P (diamond structure) P_4: mp = 44 °C bp = 280 °C
H, C, H (methane structure) CH_4: mp = −182.5 °C bp = −164 °C	O with H, H (water structure) H_2O: mp = 0 °C bp = 100 °C	S ring structure S_8: mp = 113 °C bp = 445 °C

Covalent gases, liquids and solids

The covalent bonds holding the atoms together are strong, but the **forces between the molecules are weak,** and it doesn't take a lot of energy to separate the molecules. It is these weak forces between molecules that have to be broken when a molecular substance melts or boils. This results in **molecular substances** generally having **low melting and boiling points**.

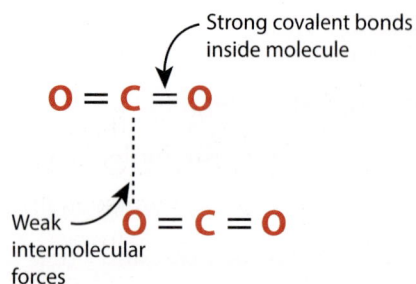

Strong covalent bonds inside molecule

$O=C=O$

Weak intermolecular forces

$O=C=O$

Covalent molecules have weak forces of attraction between them.

Covalent network

Some covalently bonded substances form giant three-dimensional structures called
covalent networks in which all the atoms are covalently bonded to each other.
There are no individual molecules. Covalent bonds are relatively strong so it takes
a lot of energy to break a covalent bond. Network substances therefore have
very high melting and boiling points. Diamond and silicon dioxide are common
examples of covalent networks.

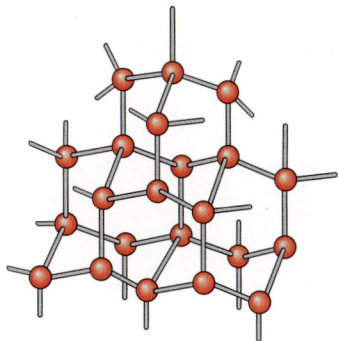

● Silicon atom

● Carbon atom
● Oxygen atom

Part of diamond's covalent network.   *Part of silicon dioxide's covalent network.*

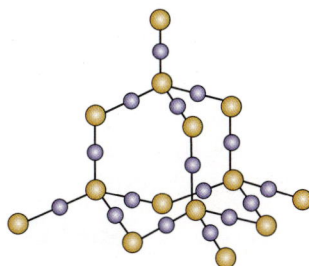

The three-dimensional network makes diamond and silicon dioxide extremely
strong – diamond is the hardest known substance. **Covalent network substances**
are generally **very strong**. Covalent substances are generally **insoluble in water**
but can be soluble in covalent liquids, such as white spirit. Covalent liquids tend
to evaporate quickly and can be very flammable. Covalent substances (with the
exception of carbon in the form of graphite) **do not conduct electricity** in any
state because they have no electrons free to move from atom to atom.

Quick Test

1. Complete the summary. You may wish to use the word bank to help you.

Covalent substances exist as either individual (a)_____ or giant (b)_____.
Many molecular substances are (c)_____or liquids. This is because although the
(d)_____ bonds that hold the atoms together are relatively (e)_____, the forces
between the molecules are (f)_____. It does not take a lot of (g)_____ to separate
the (h)_____. This results in molecular substances having (i)_____ melting
and boiling points. Covalent network substances have (j)_____ melting and boiling
points. This is because each atom in the network is (k)_____ bonded to other atoms
resulting in a very strong (l)_____ structure, which needs a lot of energy to break
the (m)_____. Covalent substances are generally (n)_____ in water but can
(o)_____ in covalent liquids. Covalent substances do not conduct (p)_____
because the (q)_____ are not free to move from atom to atom.

Word bank

three-dimensional, bonds, covalent, covalently, dissolve, electricity, electrons,
energy, gases, high, insoluble, low, molecules, networks, separate, strong, weak

Structure and properties of ionic compounds

Structure of ionic compounds

Ionic compounds form when metal atoms transfer electrons to non-metal atoms resulting in positive metal ions and negative non-metal ions. They do this to achieve the stable electron arrangement of a noble gas. The attraction of positive and negative ions is called an ionic bond.

In ionic compounds the oppositely charged positive (metal) ions and negative (non-metal) ions form a giant structure known as an **ionic lattice**. Sodium chloride (NaCl) is a good example of an ionic lattice.

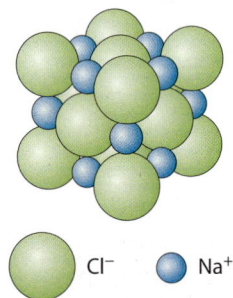

Cl⁻   Na⁺

The ions in sodium chloride form a three-dimensional lattice.

Sodium chloride crystals are cubic shaped.

There are strong **electrostatic forces** of attraction between the oppositely charged ions. This results in each ion being surrounded by ions carrying the opposite charge. A giant three-dimensional structure (ionic lattice) is produced.

Properties

Ionic compounds are solids at room temperature and have many properties in common. These properties include:

- **Electrical non-conductors as solids** – the ions are not free to move in the lattice.
- **Electrical conductors when in solution or a molten liquid** – the ions are free to move and act as charge carriers. They are attracted to the oppositely charged electrode of a d.c. supply.
- **High melting and boiling points** – it takes a lot of energy to break the ions apart.
- **Solubility in water** – the regular pattern of the ions in the lattice is broken down, and the ions are surrounded by water molecules.

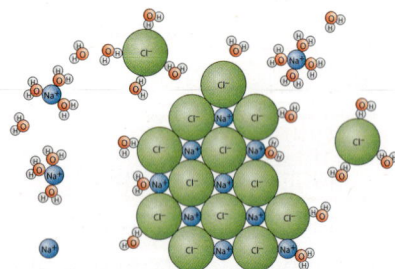

The sodium chloride crystal lattice breaks down when it dissolves in water.

Comparing ionic and covalent properties

Colour

The colour of the substance can often indicate the type of bonding – many **ionic** substances are highly coloured.

State

If a substance is a **gas or liquid** at room temperature then the substance will be **covalently** bonded and exist as individual molecules. **Solids** are more difficult to distinguish from each other. If a solid can be **easily melted**, then it will be **covalent molecular**. Wax (a hydrocarbon) melts quickly in boiling water, indicating that it is covalent molecular. The liquid wax floats on the surface of the water and doesn't dissolve, which indicates that it is covalent not ionic

The blue colour in copper sulphate crystals and the red in the gem stone ruby indicate the presence of ions.

Conductivity

Wax doesn't conduct electricity either as a solid or as a liquid, verifying that it is not ionic. The same test carried out on an ionic compound like sodium chloride, when it is in the liquid state, would show that it conducts, indicating ionic bonding.

Quick Test

1. The table shows some of the properties of potassium fluoride.

Property	
Melting point /°C	857
Boiling point /°C	1502
Electrical conductor as a solid?	no
Electrical conductor as a liquid or in solution?	yes

Suggest the type of bonding present in potassium fluoride and give two pieces of evidence from the table to support your answer.

2. A student put some solid magnesium chloride into a beaker and tested its conductivity. He concluded that magnesium chloride was covalent because it did not conduct electricity. Using your knowledge of chemistry, comment on his conclusion.

3. Sodium chloride is a solid with a melting point of 801°C, but hydrogen chloride is a gas at room temperature. Explain these observations.

Chemical formulae using group ions

Formulae of elements

Most elements have their symbol as their formula, e.g. potassium: K; magnesium: Mg; sulfur: S. The exceptions are the diatomic molecules: H_2, N_2, O_2, F_2, Cl_2, Br_2 and I_2.

Naming compounds

Compound names generally come from the names of the elements from which they are formed.

- Names ending in -**ide** usually indicates two elements in the compound.
- Names ending in -**ite** or -**ate** indicate that oxygen is also present.

Formulae of compounds using valency

Valency is another word for combining power. The valency of an element tells us how many bonds it can form with another atom. Valencies of the main group elements depend on their position in the periodic table.

Group 1	Group 2	Group 3	Group 4	Group 5	Group 6	Group 7	Group 0
H							He
Li	Be	B	C	N	O	F	Ne
Na	Mg	Al	Si	P	S	Cl	Ar
K	Ca	Ga	Ge	As	Se	Br	Kr
Valency 1	Valency 2	Valency 3	Valency 4	Valency 3	Valency 2	Valency 1	Valency 0

The 'cross over' method is the simplest way to work out formulae.

- Write the symbols for the elements.
- Work out the valency and write it under the symbols.
- Swap the numbers over.
- Cancel down to the smallest possible ratio.

Examples:

Name	hydrogen sulfide	magnesium oxide
Elements	H S	Mg O
Valency	1 2	2 2
Formula ratio	2 1	1 2 2 1
Formula	H_2S	MgO

The formulae of some compounds can be worked out from their names because they have a prefix to indicate the number of atoms: mono- = one; di- = two; tri- = three; tetra- = four; penta- = five, etc. Examples: carbon **mono**xide = CO; silicon **di**oxide = SiO_2.

What does a formula tell us?

Hydrogen sulfide and carbon monoxide are covalent compounds consisting of individual molecules, and their formulae tell us exactly how many atoms of each element are in each molecule.

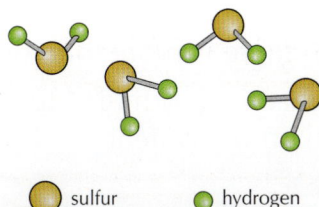

⬤ sulfur   ● hydrogen

Individual hydrogen sulfide molecules (H_2S)

Silicon dioxide is a giant covalent network – there are no molecules. Its formula tells us the ratio of the atoms of each element in the compound – SiO_2 has an Si:O ratio of 1:2 (see page 15). The ratio rule applies to all covalent network compounds.

Magnesium oxide is ionic and exists as a giant crystal lattice. Its formula tells us the ratio of the ions in the compound – MgO has an Mg:O ratio of 1:1. The ratio rule applies to all ionic compounds.

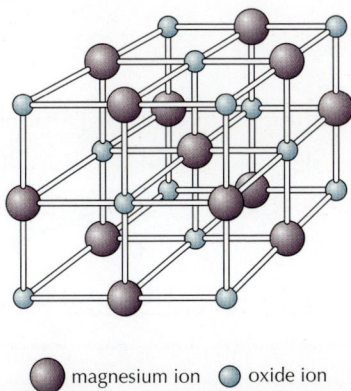

⬤ magnesium ion   ○ oxide ion

Magnesium and oxide ions arranged in a 1:1 ratio in a crystal lattice.

Formulae of compounds containing group ions

Some ions consist of more than one atom and are known as **group ions**, e.g. nitrate (NO_3^-), sulfate (SO_4^{2-}) and ammonium (NH_4^+).

The valency method can be used to work out chemical formulae for compounds containing group ions. The valency is the **number of charges** on the ion. For example the sulfate ion (SO_4^{2-}) has a 2^- charge, so its valency is 2.

> **TOP TIP**
> You don't have to memorise the group ions – they are listed in the SQA data booklet. You do need to know how to use them to work out a formula.

Examples:

Name	potassium sulfate		calcium nitrate	
Elements/group ion	K	SO_4^{2-}	Ca	NO_3^-
Valency	1	2	2	1
Formula ratio	2	1	1	2
Formula	K_2SO_4		$Ca(NO_3)_2$	

A **bracket** is always used when there is more than one group ion in a formula.

Roman numerals are used in chemical formulae to indicate the valency for elements that can have more than one valency – this is the case with many transition metals.

Examples:

Name	iron(III) carbonate		nickel(II) nitrate	
Elements/group ion	Fe	CO_3^{2-}	Ni	NO_3^-
Valency	3	2	2	1
Formula ratio	2	3	1	2
Formula	$Fe_2(CO_3)_3$		$Ni(NO_3)_2$	

When the charges are shown in the formula it is called an **ionic formula**.

> **TOP TIP**
> It is useful to learn Roman numerals up to 5:
> I = 1; II = 2; III = 3;
> IV = 4; V = 5.

Examples:

	ammonium sulfate		calcium phosphate	
Group ion:	NH_4^+	SO_4^{2-}	Ca^{2+}	PO_4^{3-}
Valency:	1	2	2	3
Formula ratio:	2	1	3	2
Ionic formula:	$(NH_4^+)_2SO_4^{2-}$		$(Ca^{2+})_3(PO_4^{3-})_2$	

A bracket is used in an ionic formula whenever there is more than one ion.

Formulae for ionic compounds can also be worked out by **balancing charges** – the overall charge on an ionic compound is neutral. For example, the charge on the ammonium ion (NH_4^+) is 1+ so when combined with the sulfate ion (SO_4^{2-}) there must be **two** NH_4^+ ions for every **one** SO_4^{2-} ion, i.e. $(NH_4^+)_2 SO_4^{2-}$. Check calcium phosphate on page 30 – overall 6+ charges are balanced by 6– charges.

TOP TIP

Be careful with name endings in ionic compounds – they can look similar but mean different things:

- Potassium sulf**ide**: the **–ide** tells us there are two ions, one is sodium so the other must be the sulfide ion – S^{2-}.
  Ionic formula: $(K^+)_2 S^{2-}$. Formula without ion charges: K_2S.
- Potassium sulf**ate**: the group ion table shows that sulfate is SO_4^{2-}.
  Ionic formula: $(K^+)_2 SO_4^{2-}$. Formula without ion charges: K_2SO_4.
- Potassium sulf**ite**: the group ion table shows that sulfite is SO_3^{2-}.
  Ionic formula: $(K^+)_2 SO_3^{2-}$. Formula without ion charges: K_2SO_3.

Quick Test

TOP TIP

Always show your working when working out a formula or doing a calculation. It lets the examiner clearly see how you got your answer.

Work out formulae for the following. Use the data in the SQA data booklet to help you – it can be downloaded from the SQA website.

1. (a) barium,   (b) fluorine
   (c) boron hydride,   (d) barium oxide
   (e) magnesium sulfide,   (f) calcium nitride
   (g) phosphorus pentachloride,   (h) nitrogen dioxide.

2. (a) sodium carbonate,   (b) magnesium sulfite,
   (c) potassium nitrate,   (d) lithium hydroxide.

3. (a) copper(II) chloride,   (b) silver(I) nitride,
   (c) iron(III) fluoride,   (d) iron(II) sulfide.

4. (a) calcium hydroxide,   (b) iron(III) sulfite,
   (c) magnesium phosphate,   (d) ammonium carbonate.

5. Write ionic formulae for 4(a)–(d) above.

Balancing chemical equations

Chemical equations

A chemical equation is a shorthand way of showing chemicals reacting and the new chemicals produced:

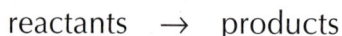

reactants → products

Chemical equations can be written in words and chemical formulae.

Example 1: Hydrogen reacts with chlorine to form hydrogen chloride.

Word equation: hydrogen   +   chlorine   →   hydrogen chloride
(diatomic element)   (diatomic element)   (compound)

Formula equation: H_2 + Cl_2 →   HCl

Example 2: Copper reacts with silver(I) nitrate solution to produce silver and copper(II) nitrate solution.

Word equation: copper + silver(I) nitrate →   silver + copper(II) nitrate

Formula equation: Cu   + $AgNO_3$ →   Ag   + $Cu(NO_3)_2$

Balanced chemical equations

In a **balanced equation** the total number of atoms of each element on the left-hand side of the equation equals the total on the right.

The equations in examples 1 and 2 are unbalanced because the number of atoms on each side of the equation is not equal.

In example 1: $H_2 + Cl_2 \rightarrow HCl$

This shows there are more hydrogen and chlorine atoms on the left-hand side than on the right. Atoms can't just disappear. The 'missing' hydrogen and chlorine atoms must have formed another hydrogen chloride molecule, as this is the only product.

An unbalanced equation.

Balancing the equation: $H_2 + Cl_2 \rightarrow 2HCl$

$$H_2 \quad + \quad Cl_2 \qquad\qquad\qquad\qquad 2HCl$$

A balanced equation.

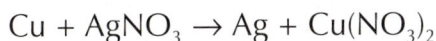

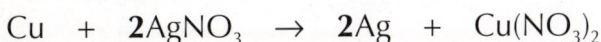

There are now the same number of atoms on each side of the equation.

When balancing an equation, numbers are put in front of formulae, never in between the symbols in the formula.

TOP TIP

Formulae are never changed in order to balance an equation.

In example 2:

Unbalanced equation: $Cu + AgNO_3 \rightarrow Ag + Cu(NO_3)_2$

The unbalanced formula equation shows that there are two NO_3 groups on the right-hand side but only one on the left-hand side. To balance the two NO_3 groups on the right-hand side a 2 has to be put in front of the $AgNO_3$ on the left-hand side.

$$Cu \quad + \quad 2AgNO_3 \quad \rightarrow \quad Ag \quad + \quad Cu(NO_3)_2$$

The equation is still not balanced because there are now two Ag on the left-hand side. This is balanced by adding a 2 in front of the Ag on the right-hand side.

Balanced equation: $Cu \quad + \quad 2AgNO_3 \quad \rightarrow \quad 2Ag \quad + \quad Cu(NO_3)_2$

Calculating quantities from balanced equations

Quantities reacting and being produced can be calculated from balanced equations. See page 65 for an example.

Quick Test

1. Write formulae equations for the following reactions:
   (a) barium chloride + magnesium sulfate → barium sulfate + magnesium chloride
   (b) iron + copper(II) nitrate → iron(II) nitrate + copper
   (c) copper(II) sulfate + sodium hydroxide → copper(II) hydroxide + sodium sulfate
2. Balance the following equations:
   (a) $Na + S \rightarrow Na_2S$
   (b) $K + O_2 \rightarrow K_2O$
   (c) $AgNO_3 + MgCl_2 \rightarrow AgCl + Mg(NO_3)_2$

Gram formula mass and the mole

Relative formula mass

The relative formula mass of a **compound**, often referred to as formula mass, can be calculated from its formula by adding together the relative atomic masses (RAM) of all the atoms shown in the formula.

- For potassium sulfate:

$$K_2 \qquad S \qquad O_4$$
$$(39 \times 2) + 32 + (4 \times 16) = 174$$

The formula mass of K_2SO_4 is **174**.

- For calcium nitrate:

$$Ca \qquad (N \quad O_3)_2$$
$$40 + ((14 + (3 \times 16)) \times 2 = 164$$

The formula mass of $Ca(NO_3)_2$ is **164**.

TOP TIP

A table of RAM values for some common elements can be found in the SQA data booklet.

TOP TIP

Setting out your working this way means you are less likely to make a mistake and clearly shows how you have worked out the answer.

The mole

In order to do chemical calculations chemists use a quantity called the mole, often shortened to **mol**.

One mole of any substance is its formula mass in grams, i.e. the **gram formula mass (GFM)**.

So, using the examples above:

1 mol of K_2SO_4 has a gram formula mass of **174 g**, i.e. **1 mol = 174 g**.

1 mol of $Ca(NO_3)_2$ has a gram formula mass of **164 g**, i.e. **1 mol = 164 g**.

It is possible to have more than one mole of a substance and also fractions of a mole.

For example, **2 mol** of K_2SO_4 = 2 x 174 = **348 g** and **0.5 mol** of K_2SO_4 = 0.5 × 174 = **87 g**.

Generally, **mol = mass / GFM**.

From this, **mass = mol × GFM**.

Example 1: Calculate the number of **moles** of $Ca(NO_3)_2$ in 196 g.

Worked answer: n = m / GFM

$$= 196 / 164$$
$$mol = 1.2 \ mol$$

TOP TIP

The SQA data booklet shows the relationship between moles (n), mass (m) and gram formula mass (GFM) as

$$n = \frac{m}{GFM}$$

Example 2: Calculate the number of **moles** of K_2SO_4 in 43.5 g

Worked answer: n = m / GFM

$$= 43.5 / 174$$

$$mol = 0.25\ mol$$

Example 3: Calculate the **mass** of K_2SO_4 in 0.45 mol.

Worked answer: m = n × GFM

$$= 0.45 × 174$$

$$mass = 78.3\ g$$

Example 4: Calculate the **mass** of 1.3 mol of $Ca(NO_3)_2$

Worked answer: m = n × GFM

$$= 1.3 × 164$$

$$mass = 213.2\ g$$

Quick Test

Check your answer to each question before moving on to the next one.

1. Calculate the gram formula mass of the following:
    (a) calcium carbonate ($CaCO_3$)
    (b) iron(III) hydroxide ($Fe(OH)_3$)
    (c) copper(II) nitrate ($Cu(NO_3)_2$)
    (d) ammonium sulfate (($NH_4)_2SO_4$)

Use your answers to 1 (a)–(d) to answer questions 2 and 3.

2. Calculate the number of moles in each of the following:
    (a) 7.5 g of $CaCO_3$
    (b) 162 g of $Fe(OH)_3$
    (c) 18.75 g of $Cu(NO_3)_2$
    (d) 231 g of $(NH_4)_2SO_4$

3. Calculate the mass of each of the following:
    (a) 2.3 mol of $CaCO_3$
    (b) 0.2 mol of $Fe(OH)_3$
    (c) 1.4 mol of $(Cu(NO_3)_2$
    (d) 0.6 mol of $(NH_4)_2SO_4$

Connecting moles, volume and concentration in solutions

Mass and moles are connected – moles can be worked out from mass and GFM, and mass from moles and GFM.

When a substance is dissolved in water, a solution is formed. The **concentration** of the dissolved substance in the solution can be worked out if the number of moles (or mass) of the dissolved substance and the volume of solution formed are known.

concentration of solution = moles of substance dissolved / volume of solution made (in **litres**)

$$C = n / V$$

From this, $n = C \times V$ and $V = n / C$

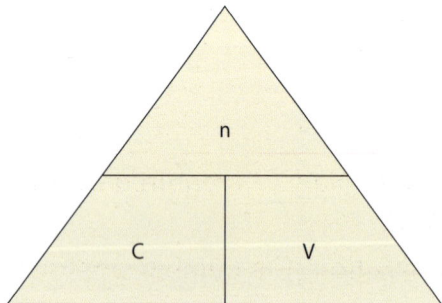

TOP TIP

You may wish to use the concentration triangle to help you remember the connection between concentration, moles and volume.

Example 1: Calculate the **concentration** of the solution formed when 0.3 mol of sodium hydroxide is dissolved in water and the volume made up to 250 cm^3.

Worked answer: C = n / V

= 0.3 / 0.25

C = 1.2 mol l^{-1}

TOP TIP

Volume must be in litres. The unit of concentration is mol l^{-1} (moles per litre).

Example 2: Calculate the number of **moles** in 50 cm^3 of a 0.1 mol l^{-1} solution of silver nitrate.

Worked answer: n = C × V

= 0.1 × 0.05

n = 0.005 mol

TOP TIP

The relationship between moles (n), concentration (C) and volume (V) is given in the SQA data booklet as:
n = CV

Example 3: Calculate the **volume** of a 0.15 mol l^{-1} solution that contains 0.45 mol of sodium chloride.

Worked answer: V = n / C

$$= 0.45 / 0.15$$

$$\textbf{V = 3.0 l}$$

Example 4: Calculate the **concentration** of a solution, in **mol l^{-1}**, of potassium hydroxide (KOH) made when 1.7 g is dissolved in water and made up to 100 cm³.

Worked answer: The answer has to be in **mol l^{-1}** so the mass in grams must first be converted to moles:

n = m / GFM   GFM of K   O   H

$$= 1.7 / 56 \qquad\qquad\qquad |\quad\; |\quad\; |$$

$$= 0.03 \text{ mol} \qquad\qquad 39 + 16 + 1 = 56 \text{ g}$$

Then, C = n / V

$$= 0.03 / 0.1$$

$$\textbf{c = 0.003 mol } \textbf{l}^{-1}$$

Example 5: Calculate the **mass** of sodium carbonate (Na_2CO_3) required to prepare 100 cm³ of a solution of concentration 0.25 mol l^{-1}.

Worked answer: In order to calculate mass in a solution, the number of moles must first be calculated.

n = C × V

$$= 0.25 \times 0.1$$

$$n = 0.025 \text{ mol}$$

Then, m = n × GFM   gfm of Na_2 C O_3

$$= 0.025 \times 106 \qquad\qquad\quad |\qquad |\qquad\quad |$$

$$\textbf{mass = 2.65 g} \qquad (2 \times 23) + 12 + (3 \times 16) = 106 \text{ g}$$

Quick Test

1. Calculate the concentration, in mol l^{-1}, of the solution formed when 0.3 mol of lithium chloride is dissolved in a little water and made up to 500 cm³ with water.

2. Calculate the concentration, in mol l^{-1}, of the solution formed when 3.5 g of potassium sulfate (GFM = 174 g) is dissolved in a little water and made up to 250 cm³ with water.

3. Calculate the number of moles in 360 cm³ of a 0.25 mol l^{-1} calcium nitrate solution.

4. Calculate the mass of ammonium nitrate (GFM = 80 g) required to prepare 250 cm³ of a solution of concentration 0.7 mol l^{-1}.

Acids and bases

pH and hydrogen ion concentration

pH is used as a way of indicating whether a solution is acid, alkali or neutral:

Acids: pH less than 7 Alkalis: pH greater than 7 Neutral: pH = 7

The pH scale runs from below zero to above 14.

pH is a measure of the hydrogen ion concentration in solution.

In water and neutral solutions a very small proportion of the water molecules break down to form equal concentrations of hydrogen ions and hydroxide ions and the pH = 7.

This is known as the **dissociation of water** and is shown as:

$$[H_2O(\ell)] \rightleftharpoons [H^+(aq)] + [OH^-(aq)] \quad [\ ] = \text{concentration}$$

The $\rightleftharpoons$ symbol shows that the reaction is reversible – as the molecules break down to form ions most rejoin to form water molecules again.

TOP TIP

Always pH, **never** Ph, PH or ph.

How do acids and alkalis form in solution?

When a **non-metal oxide** dissolves in water an acidic solution is formed. This means there is an increase in the $[H^+(aq)]$ and a decrease in the $[OH^-(aq)]$. The higher the $[H^+(aq)]$, the more acidic the solution is and the lower the pH number.

Sulfur dioxide, one of the causes of acid rain, dissolves in water to form sulfurous acid. Some of the sulfur dioxide molecules dissolve in water to give hydrogen ions and sulfite ions.

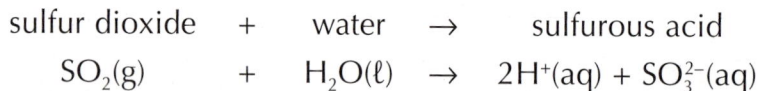

sulfur dioxide $+$ water $\rightarrow$ sulfurous acid

$$SO_2(g) + H_2O(\ell) \rightarrow 2H^+(aq) + SO_3^{2-}(aq)$$

When a **soluble metal oxide** dissolves in water an alkaline solution is formed. This means there is an increase in the $[OH^-(aq)]$ and a decrease in the $[H^+(aq)]$. The higher the $[OH^-(aq)]$ the lower the $[H^+(aq)]$ and the higher the pH number.

Sodium oxide, for example, ionises completely in water to form sodium hydroxide.

$$(Na^+)_2\, O^{2-}(s) + H_2O(\ell) \rightarrow 2Na^+(aq) + 2OH^-(aq)$$

This diagram summarises the comparison of ion concentration in acid and alkaline solutions with water.

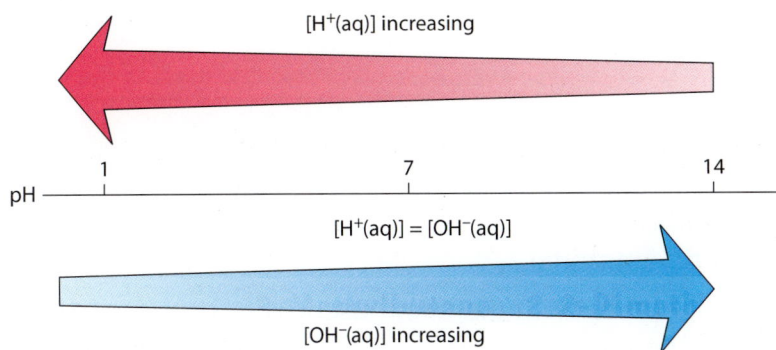

$[H^+(aq)]$ increasing

1		7	14

pH

$[H^+(aq)] = [OH^-(aq)]$

$[OH^-(aq)]$ increasing

Comparison of ion concentration in acid and alkaline solutions with water.

TOP TIP

Water and neutral solutions : $[H^+(aq)] = [OH^-(aq)]$

Acid : $[H^+(aq)]$ greater than $[OH^-(aq)]$

Alkali : $[H^+(aq)]$ less than $[OH^-(aq)]$

Diluting acids and alkalis

When water is added to an acid the acid is diluted – its concentration decreases. This means the concentration of the $H^+(aq)$ ions decrease. The pH rises towards pH 7. The solution becomes less and less acidic.

During dilution of an alkali, because the concentration of the hydroxide ions is decreasing, the pH falls towards 7. The solution becomes less and less alkaline.

Quick Test

1. Complete the following summary. You may wish to use the word bank to help you.

   In pure water and neutral solutions the concentration of (a) _____ ions is (b) _____ to the concentration of hydroxide (c) _____. When a (d) _____ oxide dissolves in water an acid solution is formed. The pH of an acid is (e) _____ 7 and the concentration of hydrogen ions is (f) _____ than the concentration of hydroxide ions. When a (g) _____ oxide dissolves in water an alkaline solution is formed. The pH of an alkaline solution is (h) _____ 7 and the concentration of hydrogen ions is (i) _____ than the concentration of hydroxide ions.

   Word bank

   above, below, equal, greater, hydrogen, ions, less, metal, non-metal

2. A solution has pH = 3.

   (a) How will be the concentration of hydrogen ions compare with the hydroxide ions in the solution?

   (b) The solution is diluted with water. Explain what will happen to the pH of the solution.

Neutralisation and volumetric titrations

Neutralisation and salt formation

In a **neutralisation** reaction an acid reacts with a base to form water and a salt, and, if the base is a carbonate, carbon dioxide is also formed. Bases are metal oxides, hydroxides, carbonates and ammonia.

The first part of the name of a salt comes from the alkali used. The second part comes from the acid as shown in the table.

Acid	Salt name ending
hydrochloric	chloride
nitric	nitrate
sulfuric	sulfate

Generally: acid + alkali → water + salt

Neutralisation and chemical equations

When an acid is neutralised the hydrogen ions are removed and replaced in solution by metal ions. Looking at the equations for neutralisation reactions helps us see exactly what is happening during the reactions.

Acid + metal hydroxide

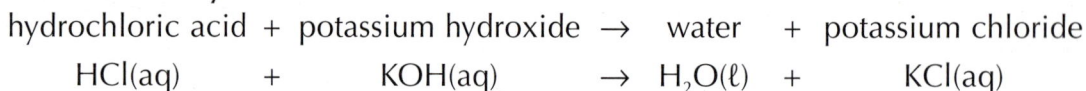

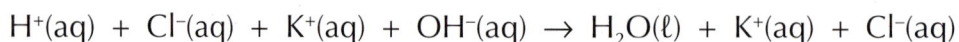

hydrochloric acid + potassium hydroxide →   water   + potassium chloride

$HCl(aq)$ + $KOH(aq)$ → $H_2O(\ell)$ + $KCl(aq)$

$H^+(aq) + Cl^-(aq) + K^+(aq) + OH^-(aq) → H_2O(\ell) + K^+(aq) + Cl^-(aq)$

Looking closely at the equation it can be seen that Cl^- and K^+ appear on both sides. This means that they have not taken part in the reaction. Ions that do not take part in a reaction are known as **spectator ions**. The ions that have taken part in the reaction are the H^+ and OH^- ions. Water is the only new product.

Rewriting the equation without the spectator ions:

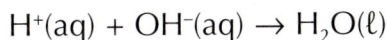

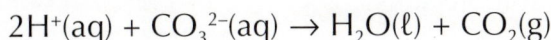

$H^+(aq) + OH^-(aq) \rightarrow H_2O(\ell)$

The equation clearly shows the $H^+(aq)$ ions being removed from solution as $H_2O(\ell)$.

Acid + metal oxide

nitric acid + sodium oxide → water + sodium nitrate

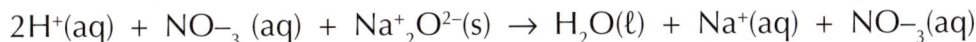

$2HNO_3(aq) \quad + \quad Na_2O(s) \quad \rightarrow \quad H_2O(\ell) \quad + \quad NaNO_3(aq)$

$2H^+(aq) + NO_3^-(aq) + Na_2^+O^{2-}(s) \rightarrow H_2O(\ell) + Na^+(aq) + NO_3^-(aq)$

Spectator ions: $Na^+(aq) + NO_3^-(aq)$ Reacting ions: $2H^+(aq) + O^{2-}(s)$

Again the equation clearly shows the $2H^+(aq)$ ions being removed from solution as $H_2O(\ell)$.

Acid + metal carbonate

sulfuric acid + lithium carbonate → water + lithium sulfate + carbon dioxide

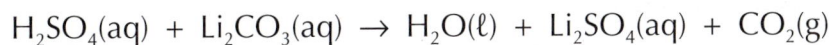

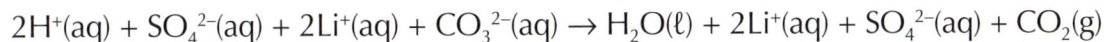

$H_2SO_4(aq) + Li_2CO_3(aq) \rightarrow H_2O(\ell) + Li_2SO_4(aq) + CO_2(g)$

$2H^+(aq) + SO_4^{2-}(aq) + 2Li^+(aq) + CO_3^{2-}(aq) \rightarrow H_2O(\ell) + 2Li^+(aq) + SO_4^{2-}(aq) + CO_2(g)$

Spectator ions: $SO_4^{2-} + Li^+$. Reacting ions: $2H^+$ and CO_3^{2-}.

Rewriting the equation without the spectator ions:

$2H^+(aq) + CO_3^{2-}(aq) \rightarrow H_2O(\ell) + CO_2(g)$

Again, the equation clearly shows the $H^+(aq)$ ions being removed from solution as $H_2O(\ell)$.

If solid lithium carbonate was used, the equation without spectator ions would be:

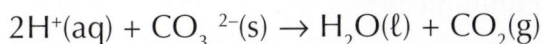

$2H^+(aq) + CO_3^{2-}(s) \rightarrow H_2O(\ell) + CO_2(g)$

Each of the acid reactions with a base clearly shows that in a neutralisation the only reaction taking place is the removal of the hydrogen ions as water.

TOP TIP

When an ionic compound is in solution the ionic lattice breaks down and the ions are free to move around. So, instead of writing the ionic formula for, say, potassium hydroxide as $K^+OH^-(aq)$, it is written as separate ions, $K^+(aq) + OH^-(aq)$.

Volumetric titrations

A neutralisation reaction between an acid and an alkali can be carried out accurately in an experiment called a **titration**.

- A titration involves using a **burette**, to gradually add accurately measured volumes of the acid into a conical flask containing alkali.
- The alkali is accurately measured using a **pipette**.
- A few drops of a chemical called an **indicator** are also added to the flask. Indicators change colour just as the neutralisation reaction is complete. This is the **end-point**.
- The volume of acid added to neutralise the alkali is then read off the scale on the side of the burette.
- The volumes of acid and alkali can then be used to calculate the unknown concentration of an acid or alkali (see page 41).

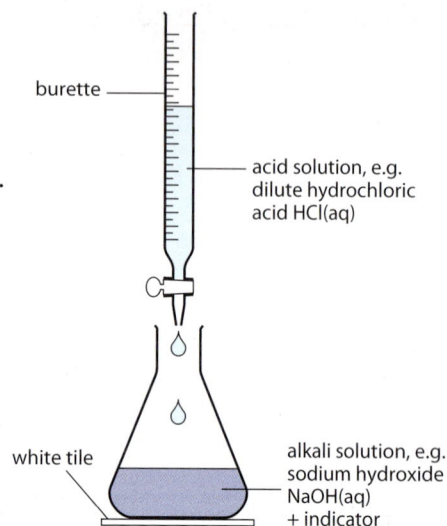

burette

acid solution, e.g. dilute hydrochloric acid HCl(aq)

white tile

alkali solution, e.g. sodium hydroxide NaOH(aq) + indicator

A diagram of acid–alkali titration.

Making soluble salts

Titrating an acid with an alkali and reacting insoluble metal oxides and carbonates (bases) with acid can be used to make soluble salts.

Method 1: Titration

1 Select the acid and alkali containing the ions needed to form the salt.

Example: For lithium chloride use lithium hydroxide solution and hydrochloric acid.

2 Carry out a volumetric titration, using an indicator.

3 Note the volume of acid at the end-point and repeat the titration without the indicator.

4 Evaporate the water from the salt solution produced to leave the solid salt.

Method 2: Reacting an insoluble base with an acid

1 Select the acid and insoluble base containing the ions needed to form the salt.

Example: For calcium nitrate use calcium carbonate and nitric acid.

2 Add the carbonate to the acid until no more carbonate reacts (no more bubbles of gas and solid carbonate is seen at the bottom of the flask).

3 Filter off the unreacted carbonate.

4 Evaporate the water from the salt solution produced to leave the solid salt.

Follow the same procedure if using an insoluble oxide – no bubbles of gas will be seen but unreacted oxide will be seen at the bottom of the flask when all the acid is neutralised.

TOP TIP

The table of solubility of compounds is found in the SQA data booklet. The advantage of using an insoluble base is that no indicator is needed as in the titration method so the reaction doesn't need repeated as it does in the titration method.

Titration calculation

The results from a volumetric titration can be used to calculate the concentration of a reactant if the concentration of the other reactant and the volume of both solutions are known.

Relationship used: $\dfrac{C_1 V_1}{n_1} = \dfrac{C_2 V_2}{n_2}$

where C_1 = concentration of reactant 1 C_2 = concentration of reactant 2

V_1 = volume of reactant 1 V_2 = volume of reactant 2

n_1 = number of moles of reactant 1 n_2 = number of moles of reactant 2
from balanced equation from balanced equation

Example 1: 20.0 cm³ of potassium hydroxide solution was neutralised by 12.0 cm³ of 0.1 mol l⁻¹ sulfuric acid. The balanced equation for the reaction is:

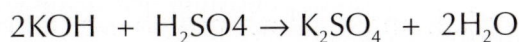

$$2KOH + H_2SO4 \rightarrow K_2SO_4 + 2H_2O$$

Calculate the **concentration** of the potassium hydroxide solution.

Answer: $\dfrac{C_1 V_1}{n_1} = \dfrac{C_2 V_2}{n_2}$

So, $\dfrac{C_1 \times 20.0}{2} = \dfrac{0.1 \times 12.0}{1}$

So, $C_1 = \dfrac{0.1 \times 12.0 \times 2}{20 \times 1}$

$C_1 = 0.12$ mol l⁻¹

Example 2: 0.1 moll^{-1} of hydrochloric acid was neutralised by 15.0 cm^3 of 0.25 moll^{-1} sodium hydroxide. The balanced equation for the reaction is:

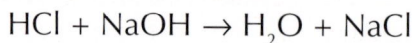

$$HCl + NaOH \rightarrow H_2O + NaCl$$

Calculate the **volume** of hydrochloric acid which reacted.

Answer: $$\frac{C_1V_1}{n_1} = \frac{C_2V_2}{n_2}$$

So, $$\frac{0.1 \times V_1}{1} = \frac{0.25 \times 15.0}{1}$$

So, $$V_1 = \frac{0.25 \times 15.0 \times 1}{1 \times 0.1}$$

$$V_1 = 37.5 \text{ cm}^3$$

TOP TIP

The relationship $\dfrac{C_1V_1}{n_1} = \dfrac{C_2V_2}{n_2}$ is in the SQA data booklet so you don't need to memorise it.

Quick Test

1. The equation shows the neutralisation of potassium hydroxide with sulfuric acid.

    $$H_2SO_4(aq) + 2KOH(aq) \rightarrow 2H_2O(\ell) + K_2SO_4(aq)$$

    (a) Rewrite the equation showing the charge on each ion.

    (b) Rewrite the ionic equation without the spectator ions to show what happens to the hydrogen ions during neutralisation.

    (c) Name the salt formed

    (d) Describe how a pure sample of the salt could be obtained.

2. Complete the following summary. You may wish to use the word bank to help you.

    To carry out a titration of an acid with an alkali, the acid is poured into a (a)_____. The alkali is drawn up into a (b)_____ and emptied into a conical flask. A few drops of (c)_____ are added to the flask. The acid is carefully added to the flask and at the neutralisation point the indicator changes (d)_____. This is the signal to stop the (e)_____. The volume of acid needed to (f)_____ the alkali is then read off the scale on the side of the burette.

    Word bank

    burette, colour, indicator, neutralise, pipette, titration

3. (a) 12 cm^3 of hydrochloric acid was neutralised by 17.0 cm^3 of 0.2 moll^{-1} potassium hydroxide. The balanced equation for the reaction is:

    $$HCl + KOH \rightarrow H2O + KCl$$

    Calculate the **concentration** of the potassium hydroxide solution.

    (b) 0.4 moll^{-1} of potassium hydroxide solution was neutralised by 19.0 cm^3 of 1.0 moll^{-1} sulfuric acid. The balanced equation for the reaction is:

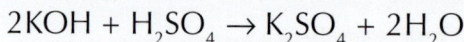

    $$2KOH + H_2SO_4 \rightarrow K_2SO_4 + 2H_2O$$

    Calculate the volume of potassium hydroxide solution which reacted.

Learning checklist

In this chapter you have learned

Rates of reaction 1

- The rate of reaction can be increased by increasing the temperature and concentration of reactants, increasing the surface area and adding a catalyst.
- Monitor rates of reaction by measuring volume of gas produced or mass of reactants used up over time.
- Draw and interpret rate of reaction graphs.

Rates of reaction 2

- the average rate of reaction = change in volume of gas / change in time or = loss in mass / change in time
- the data needed to calculate average rate can be obtained from graphs

Atoms and the periodic table

- Atoms consist of protons (p) and neutrons (n) in the nucleus with electrons (e⁻) moving around the nucleus.
- Protons have a positive charge and mass of 1.

  Neutrons have no charge and a mass of 1.

  Electrons have a negative charge and practically no mass.
- Atomic number = number of protons
- The number of protons and electrons in an atom is the same and their charges balance so the atom is neutral.
- Mass number = number of protons + number of neutrons
- Elements are arranged in the periodic table in order of their atomic number.
- Elements in the same group have the same valency and similar chemical properties.
- Electron arrangements can be found in the SQA data booklet.
- The number of outer electrons in an atom is the same as the group number of the element in the periodic table.

Nuclide notation, isotopes and relative atomic mass (RAM)

- how to use nuclide notation for an atom and ion
- most elements have isotopes – not all atoms of an element have the same number of neutrons
- relative atomic mass (RAM) is the average mass of the isotopes and can be calculated using information from a mass spectrometer

Covalent bonding and shapes of molecules

- non-metal atoms are held together in a covalent bond because of the attraction of the nucleus of one atom for the outer electrons of another
- dot and cross diagrams can be used to show how atoms share a pair of electrons to form a covalent bond

- multiple bonds can be formed between the atoms in some covalent molecules
- the specific shapes of covalent molecules can be drawn

Structure and properties of covalent substances

- covalent molecular substances have low melting and boiling points because the forces of attraction between molecules are very weak, and not a lot of energy is needed to separate the molecules
- a covalent network is a giant three-dimensional structure in which the atoms are covalently bonded to each other
- covalent network substances have high melting and boiling points because the atoms are tightly held together by strong covalent bonds, and a lot of energy is needed to break the bonds

Structure and properties of ionic compounds

- ionic compounds exist as lattices in which electrostatic attractions hold the oppositely charged ions in a three-dimensional structure
- ionic compounds have high melting and boiling points because it takes a lot of energy to break the ionic bonds
- ionic compounds do not conduct electricity when solid because the ions cannot move but do when melted or in solution because the ions are free to move towards the oppositely charged electrode in a d.c. supply
- when ionic compounds dissolve in water the electrostatic attraction between ions is replaced by attractive forces between the ions and water molecules
- many ionic compounds are highly coloured compared to covalent substances

Chemical formulae and equations

- the formula of a covalent molecular substance tells us the exact number of atoms in each molecule
- the formula of a covalent network substance or an ionic compound tells us the ratio of the atoms or ions in the substance
- how to write chemical formulae for compounds containing group ions
- how to write ionic formulae
- how to write formulae equations for compounds containing group ions
- how to balance chemical equations

Gram formula mass and the mole

- the gram formula mass of a substance is its formula mass measured in grams
- the gram formula mass of a substance is known as the mole
- how to carry out calculations involving mass into moles and moles into mass

  mass = mol × gram formula mass

  mol = mass / gram formula mass

Connecting moles, volume and concentration in solutions

- the connection between mass, volume of solutions, concentration and moles

  $C = n / V$; $n = C \times V$; $V = n / C$

Acids and bases

- pure water contains H_2O molecules and equal concentrations of $H^+(aq)$ and $OH^-(aq)$ ions
- all aqueous solutions contain $H^+(aq)$ and $OH^-(aq)$ ions
- pH is a measure of the $H^+(aq)$ ion concentration in a solution
- the concentration of $H^+(aq)$ ions in acids is higher than in water
- the concentration of $H^+(aq)$ ions in alkalis is lower than in water
- the concentration of $OH^-(aq)$ ions in alkalis is higher than in water
- the concentration of $OH^-(aq)$ ions in acids is lower than in water
- diluting acids reduces the concentration of $H^+(aq)$ so the pH of the acid increases towards 7
- diluting alkalis reduces the concentration of $OH^-(aq)$ so the pH of the alkali decreases towards 7

Neutralisation and volumetric titrations

- only the $H^+(aq)$ ions and $OH^-(aq)$ ions react in a neutralisation reaction
- a neutralisation reaction can be followed by volumetric titration
- coloured indicators are used in an acid / alkali titration to show when neutralisation has occurred
- results from titrations can be used to calculate unknown concentrations and volumes
- a titration can be repeated without an indicator to obtain the pure salt formed
- how to calculate concentration given the number of moles reacting and volume
- how to calculate volume given the number of moles reacting and the concentration of solutions

Alkanes

Alkane structures

Hydrocarbons are compounds made up of hydrogen and carbon only. Alkanes are saturated hydrocarbons with names ending in –ane. The names of straight chain alkanes can be worked out from their molecular and structural formulae.

A family of compounds that have similar chemical properties and show a trend in physical properties, e.g. boiling point, and can be represented by the same general formula, is called a **homologous series**. Alkanes are a homologous series of hydrocarbons with the **general formula C_nH_{2n+2}** where **n = 1, 2, 3**, etc.

Butane has the molecular formula C_4H_{10}. Four carbons and ten hydrogens can be arranged to give two different structures.

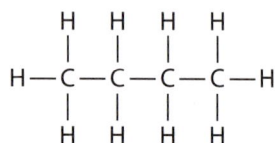

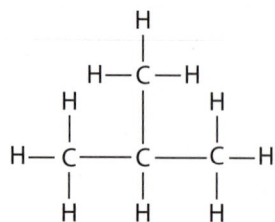

Structure 1: This arrangement is a **straight-chain** alkane.

Structure 2: This arrangement gives a **branched** alkane.

The molecules above are described as **isomers**. Their chemistry is very similar but they have different physical properties. Alkanes with more than three carbon atoms have isomers.

Shortened structural formulae can be written for the structures above.

Structure 1: $CH_3CH_2CH_2CH_3$

Structure 2: $CH_3CH(CH_3)CH_3$

Branches are shown in brackets following the carbon they are attached to.

TOP TIP

has the same structure as structure 1 so is not an isomer of 1. Although the way it is drawn makes it looks like there is a branch, there is not – what looks like a branch on the left-hand side is part of the straight chain.

Physical properties

Although the isomers of alkanes have similar chemical properties, their physical properties are different. Branching in liquid hydrocarbons causes the intermolecular forces to decrease. This means less energy is needed to separate branched molecules. This results in branched-chain isomers having **lower boiling points** and **higher volatility** than the straight-chain hydrocarbon – the more volatile a molecule is, the easier it is for it to form a gas.

Isomer	Pentane	2-Methylbutane	2,2-Dimethylpropane
Structure			
Boling point (°C)	36	27	11

Boiling points of the isomers of pentane

Using branched alkanes

Branched alkanes are particularly important in petrol manufacture where they are used to improve how smoothly the fuel burns. Petrol is a mixture of hydrocarbons in the C_5 to C_{12} range that include branched-chain alkanes, which burn more smoothly in a petrol engine than straight-chain alkanes.

The volatility of alkanes used in petrol is also important. For petrol to burn in an engine it must vaporise and mix with air. The volatility of the petrol is critical. In winter, more volatile components are added to petrol so that it vaporises more easily.

Quick Test

1. The alkanes are a **homologous series,** which can be represented by the general formula C_nH_{2n+2}. Alkanes with more than three carbon atoms have **isomers**.
   (a) Give the meaning of the terms in bold type.
   (b) Work out the formula of the alkane with nine carbon atoms.
2. Explain why a branched-chain isomer of butane has a lower boiling point than the straight-chain isomer.

Naming and drawing branched alkanes

Naming from a structural formula

Branched alkanes are named **systematically**.

1. Identify and name the longest hydrocarbon chain.
2. Identify the branches (side chains).

   For example: $-CH_3$ is **methyl**; $-C_2H_5$ is **ethyl**

3. Prefixes are used if there is more than one side chain of the same type, e.g. **di**- is used if there are two of the same type, **tri**- if there are three, etc.
4. To indicate the position of the branches on the main chain, number the carbon atoms from the end of the main chain nearer a branch.

Using these rules, the systematic name of the branched isomer of butane (see structure 2 on page 48) is:

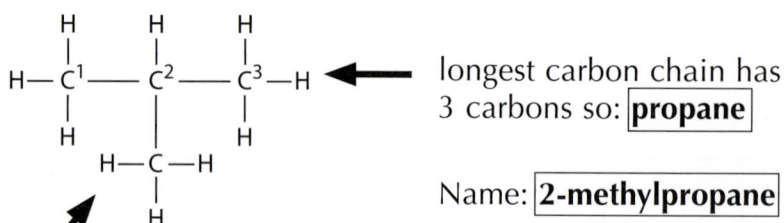

longest carbon chain has 3 carbons so: propane

Name: 2-methylpropane

methyl branch attached to 2nd carbon

Pentane, C_5H_{12}, has **three isomers**, two of which are branched. The structures and sytematic names of the branched isomers are detailed below, the first one showing how the above rules are applied:

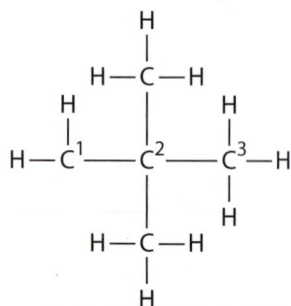

2,2-dimethylpropane

(4) (3) (2) (1)

2-methylbutane

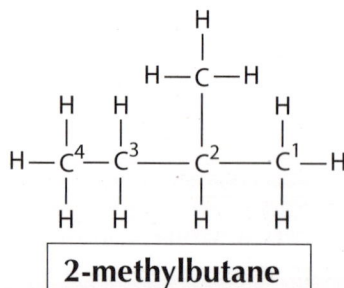

Note C atoms numbered from right-hand side to give branch lowest number

Drawing an isomer from its name

1. Identify the longest straight chain.
2. Identify the branches and how many.
3. Identify the position of the branches.

Worked example:

Draw the structure for **2,2,4-trimethylpentane**.

1. The longest straight chain is pentane – it has five carbon atoms.

C — C — C — C — C

2. There are three methyl branches: $3 \times CH_3$.

3. Two methyl groups are attached to the second carbon in the chain and one to the fourth carbon.

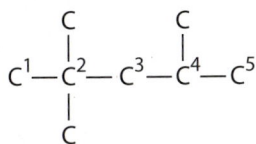

$$C^1 - C^2 - C^3 - C^4 - C^5$$

Structural formula

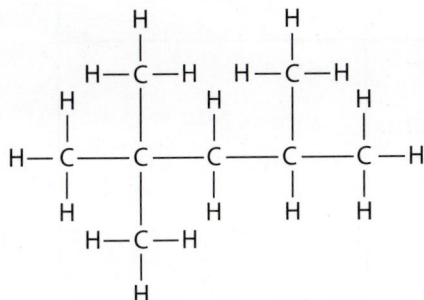

Shortened structural formula: $CH_3C(CH_3)_2CH_2CH(CH_3)CH_3$

Molecular formula: C_8H_{18}.

2,2,4-trimethylpentane is an **isomer** of octane.

Quick Test

1. The structure of a branched alkane is shown:

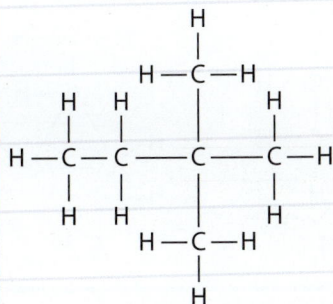

(a) Write its systematic name and shortened structural formula.

(b) Draw the structural formula and shortened structural formula for 3-methylpentane.

Cycloalkanes

As the name suggests, **cycloalkanes** are hydrocarbon compounds with the carbons arranged in a **ring**. Like the alkanes these molecules are **saturated**, i.e. the carbons are joined to each other by single carbon-to-carbon bonds. The cycloalkanes are named simply by putting the prefix cyclo- in front of the name of the straight-chain alkane with the same number of carbon atoms.

Name	Molecular formula	Structural formula	Shortened structural formula
Cyclopropane	C_3H_6		
Cyclobutane	C_4H_8		
Cyclopentane	C_5H_{10}		
Cyclohexane	C_6H_{12}		

The first four cycloalkanes

Counting carbons and hydrogens gives C_nH_{2n} as the **general formula** for cycloalkanes where **n = 3, 4, 5,** etc. Cycloalkanes with more than three carbons have **isomers** in the same homologous series, e.g. cyclobutane.

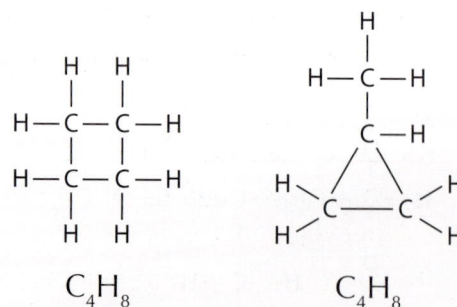

C_4H_8

C_4H_8

Cycloalkanes have the same general formula as alkenes and so are isomers, e.g. cyclopropane and propene:

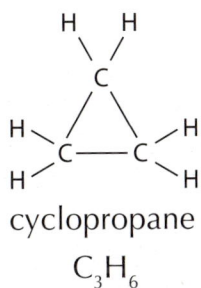

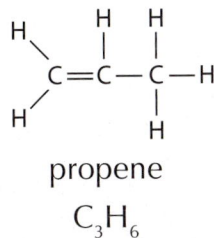

cyclopropane
C_3H_6

propene
C_3H_6

Cycloalkanes are similar to alkanes in their general chemical and physical properties, but they have higher **boiling points** and **melting points** than alkanes. This is due to stronger **forces** of attraction between the molecules because the ring shape allows for a larger area of contact.

The alkane isomers of cyclobutane are shown on page 52.

Uses of cycloalkanes

Cycloalkanes are important constituents in petrol. Like branched alkanes they burn more smoothly than straight-chain alkanes.

Other uses of cycloalkanes are: solvents for paints and varnishes, feedstocks for making other chemicals, blowing agent for making polyurethane foam.

Quick Test

1. The general formula for the cycloalkanes is C_nH_{2n}.
   (a) Work out the molecular formula for the cycloalkane with seven carbon atoms.
   (b) Name the cycloalkane with seven carbon atoms.
   (c) Draw the structural formula for the cycloalkane with seven carbon atoms.
2. (a) Draw the structural and shortened structural formulae for a cycloalkane isomer of cyclopentane.
   (b) Draw the structural formula for a possible straight-chain alkene isomer of cyclopentane.

Alkenes

Naming isomers

Alkenes are a homologous series of unsaturated hydrocarbons. Alkenes have a double C=C bond, and their name ends in –ene. General formula is C_nH_{2n} where n = 2, 3, 4 etc.

Alkenes with more than three carbons in their molecules have **isomers** in the same homologous series. Not only do they have branches, but the position of the double bond can vary.

Example: Butene has two straight-chain isomers and one branched:

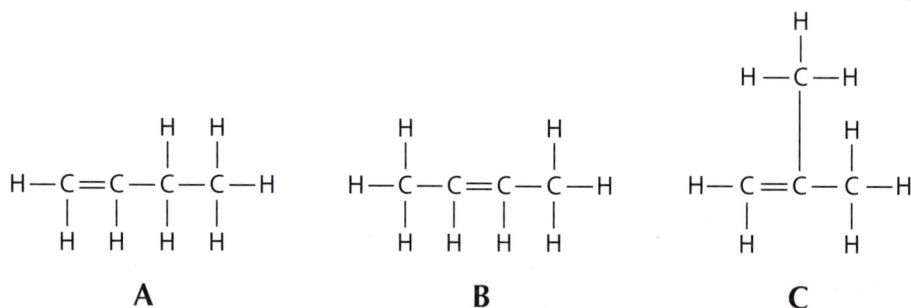

The structures are named in a similar way to alkanes, but the position of the double bond has to be included:

1. Identify the longest chain containing the double bond and name it.

2. Number the chain from the end nearer the double bond – the number of the first carbon atom with the double bond goes in the middle of the name.

3. Identify the branches (side chains) and how many there are. Prefixes are used if there is more than one side chain of the same type (di– is used if there are two of the same type, tri– if there are three, etc.).

4. Indicate the position of the branches on the main chain at the beginning of the name.

The isomers of butene, **A, B** and **C** (above), are named using the rules:

A: 1. longest chain: butene

    2. double bond on 1st carbon: **but-1-ene**

B: 1. longest chain: butene

    2. double bond on 2nd carbon: **but-2-ene**

C: 1. longest chain: propene

    2. double bond on 1st carbon: **prop-1-ene**

    3. one methyl branch: **methylprop-1-ene**

    4. methyl on 2nd carbon: **2-methylprop-1-ene**

Structural formulae from names

Example: Draw the structural formula for **2,3-dimethylpent-1-ene**.

Worked answer:

1. Identify the longest straight chain with the double bond: pent– = 5 carbons.
2. Identify the position of the double bond: pent-1-ene = between 1st and 2nd carbon.
3. Identify branches and how many: dimethyl = two methyl branches.
4. Identify the position of the branches: 2,3- = on 2nd and 3rd carbons.

Structural formula:

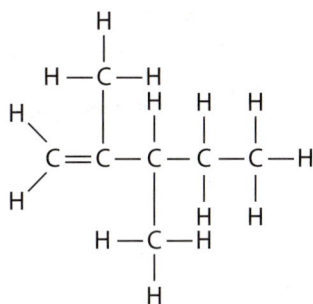

Shortened structural formula: $CH_2C(CH_3)CH(CH_3)CH_2CH_3$

Molecular formula: C_7H_{14}

Alkenes and cycloalkanes have the same general formula (C_nH_{2n}), so can be isomers. Cyclobutane (C_4H_8) would be a fourth isomer of butene (C_4H_8).

Quick Test

1. The structural formulae for three isomers of hexene (A, B and C) are shown:

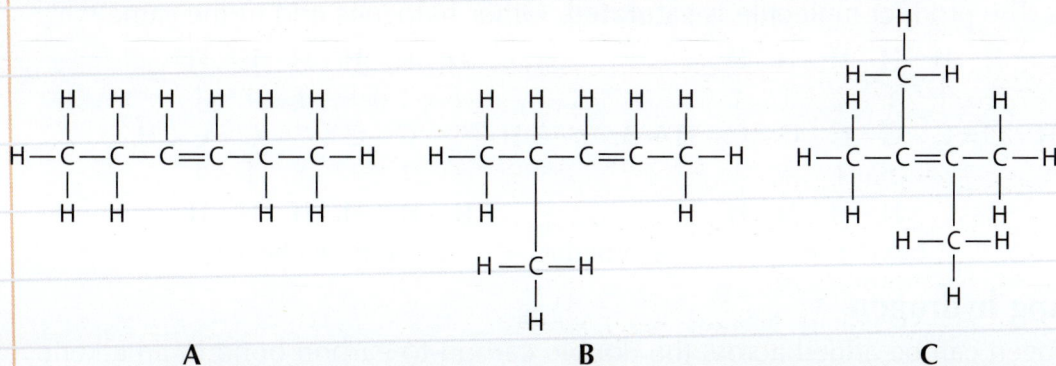

A   B   C

(a) Write systematic names and shortened structural formulae for A, B and C.

(b) Draw the structural formula for the isomer 3,3-dimethylbut-1-ene.

Reactions of alkenes

Addition reactions

Alkenes are **very reactive** due to the presence of the C=C double bond in the molecules. They are therefore important starting materials (feedstocks) in the chemical industry, used to make other important chemicals.

Reaction with halogens

Alkenes can be distinguished from alkanes using **bromine solution**.

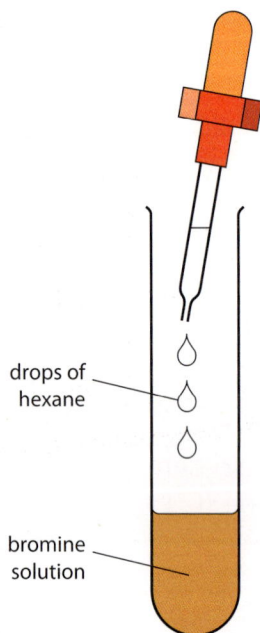

drops of hexane

bromine solution

Very slow reaction with the saturated alkane. The bromine solution stays orange-brown for some time

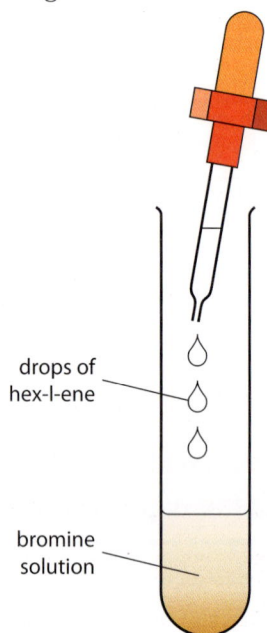

drops of hex-l-ene

bromine solution

Addition reaction with the unsaturated alkene. The bromine solution loses its colour rapidly

Comparing the reaction of hexane and hex-1-ene with bromine solution.

The reaction of hex-1-ene with bromine is an example of an **addition reaction** – the bromine atoms have added to the alkene. One of the bonds of the carbon-to-carbon double bond is broken and new atoms (or groups) join to the carbon chain. The product molecule is **saturated.** Other halogens add in the same way.

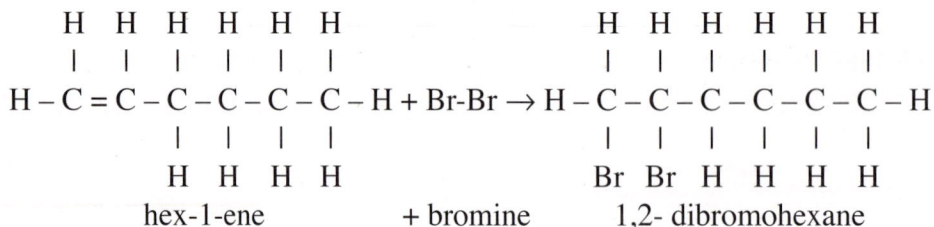

$$
\begin{array}{c}
\text{H} \quad \text{H} \quad \text{H} \quad \text{H} \quad \text{H} \quad \text{H} \\
|\quad\; |\quad\; |\quad\; |\quad\; |\quad\; | \\
\text{H} - \text{C} = \text{C} - \text{C} - \text{C} - \text{C} - \text{C} - \text{H} + \text{Br-Br} \rightarrow \\
|\quad\; |\quad\; |\quad\; | \\
\text{H} \quad \text{H} \quad \text{H} \quad \text{H} \\
\text{hex-1-ene} \qquad\qquad + \text{bromine}
\end{array}
$$

$$
\begin{array}{c}
\text{H} \quad \text{H} \quad \text{H} \quad \text{H} \quad \text{H} \quad \text{H} \\
|\quad\; |\quad\; |\quad\; |\quad\; |\quad\; | \\
\text{H} - \text{C} - \text{C} - \text{C} - \text{C} - \text{C} - \text{C} - \text{H} \\
|\quad\; |\quad\; |\quad\; |\quad\; |\quad\; | \\
\text{Br} \quad \text{Br} \quad \text{H} \quad \text{H} \quad \text{H} \quad \text{H} \\
\text{1,2- dibromohexane}
\end{array}
$$

Adding hydrogen

Hydrogen can be added across the double carbon-to-carbon bond in an alkene (unsaturated) giving the corresponding alkane (saturated). The process is also known as **hydrogenation**.

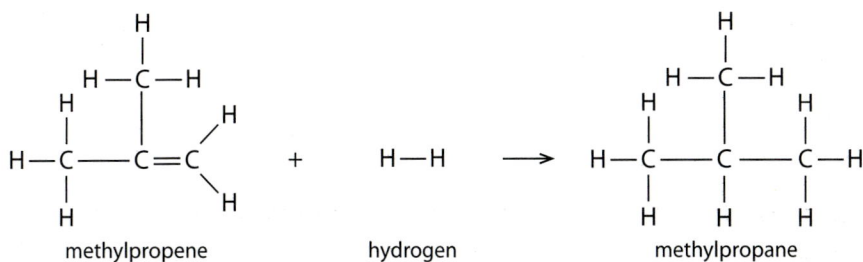

methylpropene   hydrogen   methylpropane

Adding water

The addition reaction, which involves adding water across a double carbon-to-carbon bond to form an alcohol, is also referred to as **hydration**.

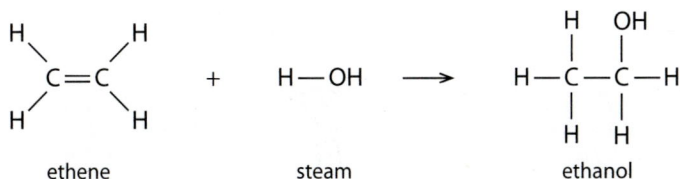

ethene   steam   ethanol

Making plastics

The most important use of alkenes is as feedstocks in the plastics industry. This is dealt with fully in Chemistry in society: Plastics.

TOP TIP

When alkenes react, the reactants always add to the carbons with the double bond.

TOP TIP

Alkanes, alkenes and cycloalkanes are all insoluble in water.

Quick Test

1. Pent-1-ene reacts with chlorine to form 1,2-dichloropentane.

$$C_5H_{10} + Cl_2 \rightarrow C_5H_{10}Cl_2$$

(a) Draw structural formulae to show how the chlorine molecule reacts with pent-1-ene.

(b) Name this type of reaction.

2. (a) But-1-ene reacts with hydrogen in an addition reaction.

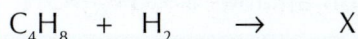

$$C_4H_8 + H_2 \rightarrow X$$

(i) Give another name for this reaction.

(ii) Write the molecular formula for compound X and name it.

(iii) To which homologous series does X belong?

(b) But-1-ene also reacts with steam in an addition reaction to produce compound Y.

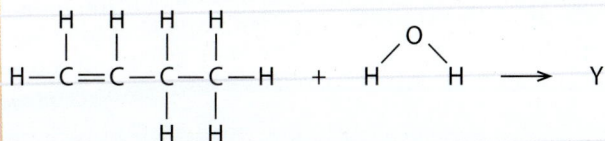

(i) Give another name for this reaction.

(ii) Draw a possible structure for the compound Y.

Alcohols

Ethanol is the second member of a **homologous series** of **alcohols**, known as alkanols.

The names and formulae of the alkanols are related to the names and formulae of the corresponding alkanes. In the alcohols a hydrogen in the alkane molecule has been replaced by an oxygen bonded to hydrogen. This is known as a **hydroxyl group (–OH)**. All alcohols contain a hydroxyl group. This is the **functional group** for alcohols and is responsible for the similarities in properties of the members of the homologous series. The 'e' from the end of the alkane name is replaced with 'ol' to give the name of the alcohol.

> **TOP TIP**
> Don't mix up the names hydroxide and hydroxyl. Hydro**xide** is the **OH⁻ ion**. Hydro**xyl** is the **–OH group**.

Alkane	Molecular formula	Alcohol	Molecular formula	Structural formula
Methane	CH_4	Methan**ol**	CH_3OH	H—C—OH (with H above and below C)
Ethane	C_2H_6	Ethan**ol**	C_2H_5OH	H—C—C—O—H (each C with H above and below)
Propane	C_3H_8	Propan**ol**	C_3H_7OH	H—C—C—C—OH (each C with H above and below)

Names and formulae for alcohols based on the corresponding alkanes

From the information in the table the general formula for the alcohols can be worked out. The general formula for the alcohols based on alkanes is $C_nH_{2n+1}OH$.

Naming alcohol isomers

> **TOP TIP**
> Alcohols have straight-chain and branched-chain isomers but you do not need to be able to draw or name branched structures.

Alcohols with more than two carbon atoms have isomers – the position of the hydroxyl group can change. There are two isomers of propanol, C_3H_7OH.

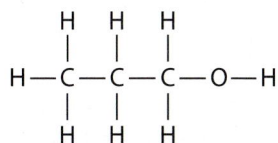

Full structural formulae

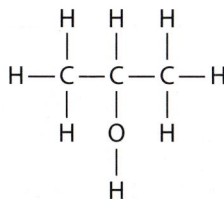

Structure 1 — H—C—C—C—O—H with H's

Structure 2

Shortened structural formulae

$CH_3CH_2CH_2OH$ $CH_3CH(OH)CH_3$

The name of an alcohol specifies where the hydroxyl group is attached to the carbon chain. The rules for naming are similar to those for naming alkenes (see page 52) but here the -OH group is given the lowest number.

TOP TIP

You will find it helpful when naming alcohols to know the names of the first eight alkanes.

Structures 1 and 2 can be named systematically.

Structure 1:

1. longest chain: propanol
2. hydroxyl on 1st carbon: **propan-1-ol**

Structure 2:

1. longest chain: propanol
2. hydroxyl on 2nd carbon: **propan-2-ol**

Formulae can be worked out from systematic names.

Worked example for **pentan-2-ol**.

1. The longest straight chain with the hydroxyl group = pentanol = 5 carbons.
2. The position of the hydroxyl group: 2 = 2nd carbon.

Structural formula:

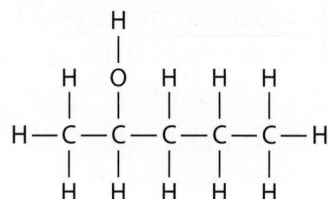

Shortened structural formula: $CH_3CH(OH)CH_2CH_2CH_3$

Molecular formula: $C_5H_{11}OH$

Quick Test

1. Draw the structural formulae for the two straight chain isomers of butanol (C_4H_9OH) and name them.
2. Draw the structural formula for hexan-3-ol and work out its molecular formula.

Properties and uses of alcohols

Properties

The alcohols are a homologous series, so show a gradual change in physical properties. The table shows the trend in melting and boiling points for straight-chain alcohols with the hydroxyl group attached to an end carbon of the chain.

Alcohol	Shortened structural formula	Melting point/°C	Boiling point/°C
Methanol	CH_3OH	−98	65
Ethanol	CH_3CH_2OH	−117	78
Propan-1-ol	$CH_3CH_2CH_2OH$	−127	97
Butan-1-ol	$CH_3(CH_2)_2CH_2OH$	−90	116
Pentan-1-ol	$CH_3(CH_2)_3CH_2OH$	−79	137

Melting points and boiling points of the first five alcohols

Explaining the trend in boiling points

The boiling points of the alcohols increase as the number of carbon atoms in the molecules increases. The longer the hydrocarbon chains, the greater the forces of attraction between molecules. This means more energy will be required to separate bigger molecules and so boiling points will increase.

There are other forces of attraction between alcohol molecules that are not present in alkanes of similar mass. This is due to the hydroxyl groups in alcohols. This results in alcohols having higher boiling points than alkanes of similar mass.

Propane: C_3H_8 **(formula mass: 44)**   **Ethanol:** C_2H_5OH **(formula mass: 46)**

bp = −44°C   bp = 78°C

Solubility in water

Small alcohol molecules like methanol and ethanol are very soluble and mix completely with water. For a molecule to dissolve in water it must be able to interact with water molecules. The presence of the –OH group on the alcohol results in strong forces of attraction forming between it and the –OH groups on the water molecules and so the small alcohol molecules mix easily with the water. The diagram shows how methanol molecules interact with water molecules:

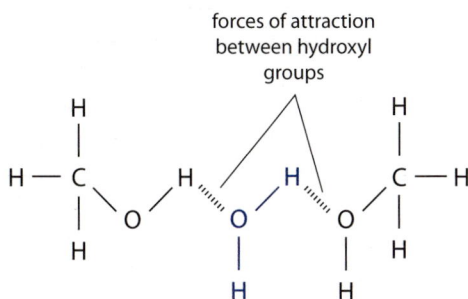

forces of attraction
between hydroxyl
groups

In **larger** alcohol molecules like octan-1-ol, the forces of attraction between the hydrocarbon parts of the alcohol molecules are stronger than the forces between the –OH groups, which makes it more difficult for large alcohol molecules to dissolve in water. The graph shows how the solubility of alcohols decreases as the number of carbon atoms in the molecule increases.

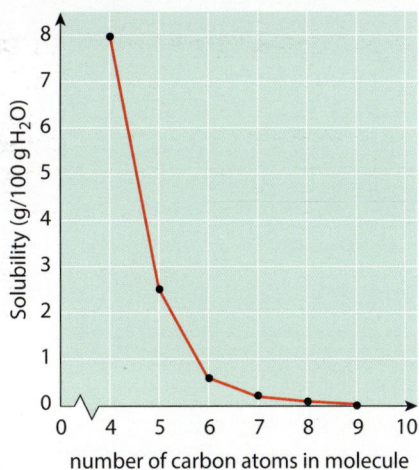

Variation in solubility of alcohols.

Extending the graph to include ethanol (C_2H_5OH) would show it to have a high solubility in water. Alcoholic drinks such as whisky contain ethanol diluted with water.

6262

GOTIT?IT?IT?

Uses of alcohols

Fuels

Alcohols are extremely flammable and can be used as fuels. Methanol and ethanol burn cleanly to give carbon dioxide and water.

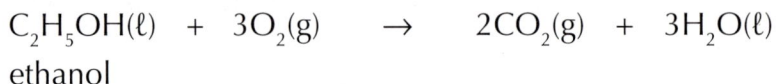

$$C_2H_5OH(l) + 3O_2(g) \rightarrow 2CO_2(g) + 3H_2O(l)$$
ethanol

Both methanol and ethanol can by used as fuels in car engines. Ethanol can be made by fermenting sugar cane, which is a renewable energy source.

Solvents

Ethanol is an effective solvent. After water it is the most important solvent used by industry.

Ethanol, as well as being used extensively in industry, is a common solvent in perfumes, food flavourings and many medical preparations.

Propan-2-ol dissolves a wide range of compounds and is used in cleaning fluids to dissolve oils. It is used to clean computer keyboards and monitor screens. It evaporates quickly and is relatively non-toxic, compared to some other solvents.

Propan-2-ol is also the alcohol used in many hand gels and disinfectant wipes.

Quick Test

1. Look at the table of melting and boiling points of the alcohols.
   (a) Predict the boiling point of hexan-1-ol.
   (b) Explain the trend in the boiling points of the alcohols.
2. Explain why nonan-1-ol ($C_9H_{17}OH$) is insoluble in water but methanol is very soluble.
3. Methanol and ethanol can be used as fuels.
   (a) State two reasons for using ethanol as a fuel.
   (b) Write a balanced equation for the combustion of methanol.
   (c) State one other use for alcohols.

Carboxylic acids

Carboxylic acids

<mark>Carboxylic acids</mark> are a homologous series that contain the **carboxyl group**, **–COOH**. The structure of the carboxyl group is:

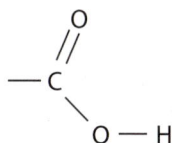

$$-C\overset{\displaystyle O}{\underset{\displaystyle O-H}{<}}$$

The carboxyl group occurs at the end of a chain of carbons.

The general formula for the carboxylic acids based on alkanes can be written as $C_nH_{2n+1}COOH$ where **n = 0, 1, 2 etc.**

Using the general formula, the first carboxylic acid in the series (n=0) has the molecular formula **HCOOH**. The name is based on the corresponding alkane. The 'e' is dropped and replaced with '–oic acid': **methanoic acid**.

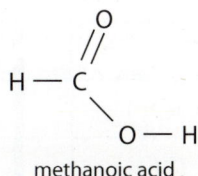

$$H-C\overset{\displaystyle O}{\underset{\displaystyle O-H}{<}}$$

methanoic acid

The second member of the series, when n=1, the molecular formula is: **CH$_3$COOH**. The molecule has two carbon atoms so the name is **ethanoic acid**:

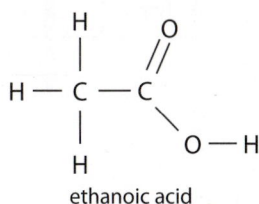

ethanoic acid

TOP TIP

The carboxyl group has a carbon atom in it, which must be included when working out the name of a carboxylic acid.

Using carboxylic acids

A major use of **methanoic acid** is as a **preservative** and **antibacterial** agent in farm animal feed. Methanoic acid is also known as formic acid. The name comes from 'formica', the latin for ant. Ant and bee stings contain this acid.

Vinegar is probably the most well-known substance to contain a carboxylic acid. Vinegar is a solution of **ethanoic acid** (CH_3COOH) in water. It is widely used as a food preservative and flavouring, and in household cleaners.

Properties

Like the alcohols, straight-chain carboxylic acids show a gradual change in some physical properties.

Carboxylic acid	Shortened structural formula	Melting point and boiling point/°C	Solubility in water/g l^{-1}
Methanoic acid	HCOOH		
Ethanoic acid	CH_3COOH		
Propanoic acid	CH_3CH_2COOH		
Butanoic acid	$CH_3(CH_2)_2COOH$	Increasing	Decreasing
Pentanoic acid	$CH_3(CH_2)_3COOH$		
Hexanoic acid	$CH_3(CH_2)_4COOH$		
Heptanoic acid	$CH_3(CH_2)_5COOH$		
Octanoic acid	$CH_3(CH_2)_6COOH$		

Variation in boiling point and solubility of carboxylic acids

Melting point/Boiling point: as the molecules get bigger, the forces of attraction between the molecules increase. This means the amount of energy needed to separate the molecules increases so the melting points and boiling points increase.

Solubility: small carboxylic acid molecules such as methanoic acid are very soluble and mix completely with water. The small molecules are able to interact with water molecules. In **larger** carboxylic acid molecules, such as octanoic acid, the long hydrocarbon part of the molecules makes it more difficult for them to dissolve in water.

Carboxylic acids react with alkalis to form water and a salt.

carboxylic acid + alkali → water + salt

ehtanoic acid + sodium hydroxide → water + sodium ehtanoate

Quick Test

1. The structural formula for a carboxylic acid is shown:

   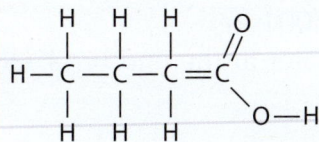

   (a) Name the carboxylic acid.

   (b) Write the molecular formula for the carboxylic acid.

2. Propanoic acid is a carboxylic acid.

   (a) Write the molecular formula for propanoic acid.

   (b) Draw the structural formula for propanoic acid.

   (c) Propanoic acid is very miscible with water but octanoic acid has very low solubility. Explain why this is the case.

3. Name the first two carboxylic acids and give a use for each.

Energy and chemicals from fuels

Calculating energy

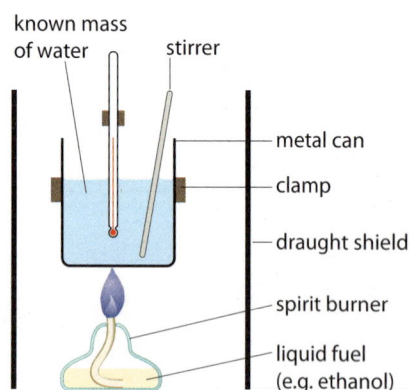

When fuels burn they give out energy – an **exothermic** reaction takes place. The fuel reacts with oxygen from the air – this is **combustion**.

$$C_2H_5OH(\ell) + 3O_2(g) \rightarrow 2CO_2(g) + 3H_2O(\ell)$$
ethanol

$$CH_4(g) + 2O_2(g) \rightarrow CO_2(g) + 2H_2O(\ell)$$
methane

When energy is taken in from the surroundings during a chemical reaction an **endothermic** reaction is said to take place.

The energy given out when a fuel burns can be calculated experimentally using a **calorimeter**. Industrial calorimeters can give very accurate measurements of the energy produced. In the lab a simple calorimeter can be made but it is not very accurate, mainly because of heat loss to the surroundings and the copper can.

Simple laboratory calorimeter.

The energy given out (E_h) when a measured mass of fuel burns and heats a known mass of water (m) can be calculated by measuring the temperature rise of the water (ΔT) and using the equation:

$E_h = c\ m\ \Delta T$ (c is the specific heat capacity of water = 4.18 kJ kg^{-1} °C^{-1})

Example: Calculate the energy transferred to the water when 1.0 g of ethanol burns, given the following experimental data:

Mass of water = 300 g (0.300 kg) (1 cm^3 of water = 1 g = 0.001 kg)
Temperature of water at the start = 20°C   Temperature of water at the end = 44°C

Worked answer:
c = 4.18   m = 0.300 ΔT = 44 − 20 = 24

Substituting values into the equation: $E_h = c\ m\ \Delta T$ = 4.18 × 0.300 × 24 E_h = **30.10 kJ**

Because of the loss of energy to the surroundings experimental values are always much lower than data booklet values.

If 1 g quantities of different fuels are burned in the same way they can be compared to see which gives out most energy.

Calculating masses reacting and produced

As well as comparing the amount of energy given out when different fuels burn, the mass of carbon dioxide given off when a fuel burns and the mass of oxygen required to completely burn a fuel can be calculated.

Example 1: Calculate the mass of carbon dioxide given off when 1 g of methanol is burned.

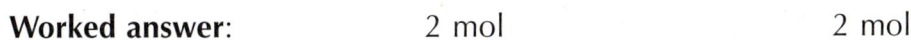

Balanced equation: $\quad\quad 2CH_3OH(\ell) + 3O_2(g) \rightarrow 2CO_2(g) + 4H_2O(\ell)$

Worked answer: $\quad\quad\quad\quad$ 2 mol $\quad\quad\quad\quad\quad\quad\quad\quad$ 2 mol

So, $\quad\quad$ 1 mol $\quad\quad \rightarrow \quad\quad$ 1 mol

Changing to grams $\quad\quad$ 32 g (GFM) $\quad \rightarrow \quad$ 44 g (GFM)

$$1\,g\left(\frac{32}{32}\right) \quad \rightarrow \quad \frac{44}{32} = \textbf{1.38 g}$$

Example 2: Calculate the mass of oxygen required to burn 50 g of methane.

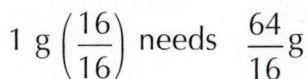

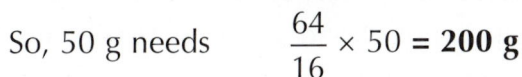

Balanced equation: $CH_4(g) + 2O_2(g) \rightarrow CO_2(g) + 2H_2O(\ell)$

Worked answer: $\quad$ 1 mol $\quad\quad\quad$ 2 mol

Changing to grams $\quad$ 16 g needs $\quad$ 64 g

$$1\,g\left(\frac{16}{16}\right) \text{ needs } \frac{64}{16}\,g$$

$$\text{So, 50 g needs} \quad \frac{64}{16} \times 50 = \textbf{200 g}$$

Quick Test

1. The experimental results below are obtained when a group of students burn 1 g of methanol (CH_3OH) in a simple laboratory calorimeter.

   Volume of water = 100 cm³

   Temperature of water at the start = 20°C　　　Temperature of water at the end = 53.5°C

   (a) Calculate the energy transferred to the water.

   (b) The energy transferred in the laboratory experiment carried out by the students is much less than the values found in the data book. Suggest why this might be the case.

   (c) Look at the diagram of the simple calorimeter. Explain why a draught shield is used and a copper beaker rather than a glass one.

2. Calculate the mass of carbon dioxide produced when 50 g of ethanol (C_2H_5OH) is burned completely.

   Balanced equation: $C_2H_5OH(\ell) + 3O_2(g) \rightarrow 2CO_2(g) + 3H_2O(\ell)$

Learning checklist

In this chapter you have learned:

- a homologous series is a group of compounds with similar chemical properties and physical properties that show a gradual change and can be represented by a general formula
- isomers are compounds with the same molecular formula but different structural formulae

Alkanes

- hydrocarbons are compounds containing hydrogen and carbon only
- the alkanes are a homologous series of hydrocarbons with general formula C_nH_{2n+2}, where n = 1, 2, 3, etc.
- alkanes have branched-chain isomers
- alkanes are generally unreactive but burn and are used as fuels

Naming and drawing branched alkanes

- how to name branched-chain alkanes, given their structure, and draw structural formulae, given the name of an alkane

Cycloalkanes

- cycloalkanes are a homologous series of saturated hydrocarbons where the carbons are joined in a ring and have a general formula C_nH_{2n} where n = 3, 4, etc.
- how to name cycloalkanes
- how to draw isomers of the cycloalkanes
- the cycloalkanes are present in petrol and are used as solvents

Alkenes

- that alkenes are a homologous series of hydrocarbons with general formula C_nH_{2n}, where n = 2, 3, 4, etc.
- alkenes have straight-chain and branched-chain isomers
- how to name alkenes systematically

Reactions of alkenes

- the C═C double bond in alkenes makes them more reactive than alkanes
- the alkenes can undergo addition reactions when other molecules join by adding across the double bond
- alkenes decolourise bromine solution very quickly in an addition reaction because alkenes are unsaturated, while alkanes only decolorise bromine solution very slowly because they are saturated and do not undergo addition reactions

Alcohols
- that alcohols are a homologous series of compounds containing the hydroxyl (–OH) functional group
- the general formula for the alcohols is $C_nH_{2n+1}OH$, where n = 1, 2, 3, etc.
- to write molecular formulae and draw structural formulae for straight-chain alcohols, given their systematic name
- to systematiclly name straight-chain alcohols, given their shortened or full structural formulae

Properties and uses of alcohols
- the melting points and boiling points of alcohols increase as they get bigger
- the solubility of alcohols decreases as they get bigger
- alcohols are very good solvents
- alcohols burn with a very clean flame and can be used as fuels

Carboxylic acids
- carboxylic acids are a homologous series of compounds containing the carboxyl (–COOH) functional group
- the general formula for the carboxylic acids is $C_nH_{2n+1}OH$, where n = 0, 1, 2, etc.
- to write molecular formulae and draw structural formulae for straight-chain carboxylic acids, given their name
- to name straight-chain carboxylic acids, given their shortened or full structural formulae
- vinegar is a solution of ethanoic acid in water
- vinegar can be used as a preservative

Energy and chemicals from fuels
- combustion, burning of fuels, is an exothermic process – heat energy is given out
- endothermic reactions take in energy from their surroundings
- fuels can be compared by measuring the energy given out when they are burned
- when a burning fuel is used to heat water the energy transferred is calculated using the formula $E_h = cm\Delta T$
- balanced equations can be used to calculate the masses of reactants and products of a reaction
- carry out calculations using balanced equations

Metals from ores

Percentage composition by mass

An **ore** is a type of rock that contains important elements including metals. Some common ores that metals can be extracted from are haematite (Fe_2O_3), chalcocite (Cu_2S) and cinnebar (HgS).

The % by mass of a metal in a compound can be calculated from its formula.

Example: Cu_2S

$$\% \text{ composition by mass of Cu} = \frac{\text{mass of Cu in formula}}{\text{formula mass of } Cu_2s} \times 100$$

$$= \frac{(2 \times 63.5)}{(2 \times 63.5) + (1 \times 32)} \times 100$$

$$= \frac{127}{159} \times 100$$

% composition by mass of Cu = 79.9%

> **TOP TIP**
> The relationship used to caluclate % by mass is given in the SQA data booklet as: % by mass = m/GFM x 100 so you don't need to memorise it.

Extraction of metals from their ores

Heating

Some metals, like gold, can be found uncombined in the Earth's crust but most metals exist as compounds in an ore.

Metals **low in reactivity**, such as silver, can be obtained simply by **heating** their ore. Ores often contain metal oxides.

If silver(I) oxide is heated, silver metal is produced:

$$2Ag_2O(s) \rightarrow 4Ag(s) + O_2(s)$$

The metal ore is said to have been **reduced** to the metal.

During the reaction the positive silver ions change to atoms by gaining an electron. This can be seen in the ionic equation:

$$2(Ag^+)_2O^{2-}(s) \rightarrow 4Ag(s) + O_2(s)$$

The positive silver ion has gained an electron and formed the metal atom. Gain of electrons is called **reduction**.

This can be shown in an **ion-electron equation**. Ion-electron equations show the electrons gained or lost by an atom or ion.

$$Ag^+(s) + e^- \rightarrow Ag(s) \qquad \text{reduction}$$

> **TOP TIP**
> The SQA data booklet gives a list of commonly used ion-electron equations.

Smelting

Some ores that are too reactive to be reduced by heat alone can be reduced by heating with carbon. This process is called **smelting**.

One of the most important examples of smelting is the extraction of iron from iron ore in a blast furnace. The diagram summarises what happens in the blast furnace. The coke loaded in at the top provides the carbon for the reaction.

iron ore, coke and limestone

(3) $Fe_2O_3 + 3CO \rightarrow 2Fe + 3CO_2$

(2) $CO_2 + C \rightarrow 2CO$

(1) $C + O_2 \rightarrow CO_2$

blast of hot air

blast of hot air

molten slag

molten iron

Iron is extracted from its ore in a blast furnace.

The ionic equation for the reduction of iron(III) oxide shows the Fe^{3+} ion being **reduced** to Fe:

$$(Fe^{3+})_2(O^{2-})_3(s) + 3CO(g) \rightarrow 2Fe(\ell) + 3CO_2(g)$$

The ion-electron equation can be written for the reduction of the iron ions:

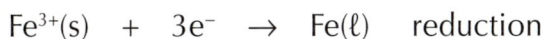

$$Fe^{3+}(s) + 3e^- \rightarrow Fe(\ell) \quad \text{reduction}$$

The carbon monoxide causes the reduction so is known as the **reducing agent**.

Reducing agents give up electrons allowing substances being reduced to gain electrons.

Using electricity

Some metals are too reactive to be reduced by chemical means. Electricity has to be used. A **direct current (dc)**, which gives a positive and negative electrode, has to be used so that the products can be identified. The positive ions are attracted to the negative electrode where they gain electrons, i.e. they are reduced. This process is known as **electrolysis**.

Aluminium is an important metal extracted from its oxide (ore) by passing a dc current through it:

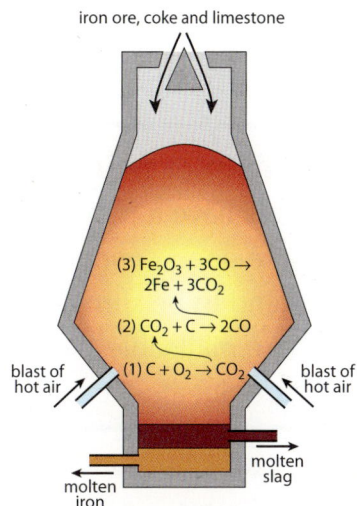

$$Al^{3+}(\ell) + 3e^- \rightarrow Al(\ell) \quad \text{reduction}$$

TOP TIP

The reactivity series (see page 73) will help you to decide which method is needed to extract the metal from its compound. Metals below copper can be extracted by heat alone. Metals above zinc need electricity. Metals in the middle can be reduced by heating with carbon.

Quick Test

1. | Calculate the percentage composition by mass of mercury in mercury sulfide (HgS).

2. | Copper can be extracted from its oxide by heating the oxide and passing carbon monoxide over it. The equation is shown:

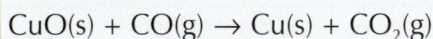

$$CuO(s) + CO(g) \rightarrow Cu(s) + CO_2(g)$$

   (a) What name is given to the process of extracting a metal in this way?

   (b) Write the ion-electron equation to show what happens to the copper(II) ion.

   (c) Identify the reducing agent.

Properties and reactions of metals

> **Remember from National 4!**
>
> Metals have a number of properties in common:
>
> - are good conductors of heat and electricity
> - tend to be shiny – have metallic lustre
> - are malleable – can be shaped
> - are ductile – can be stretched into wires.

Metallic bonding

The properties of metals can be explained by the bonding within the metals.

In metals the outer electrons of the atoms can move easily from atom to atom. The electrons within the structure are said to be **delocalised**. Metal structures can be described as 'positive ions in a sea of electrons'.

The structure is held together by metallic bonds. These are the attractive forces of the metal nuclei for the delocalised electrons moving between them. The direction of the bonds is not fixed because the electrons are moving, unlike in covalent compounds where the electrons are localised in bonds. This means that the atoms will be able to move in relation to each other and explains why the metals can be rolled into thin sheets or drawn into wires.

positive metal ions   sea of negative electrons

Metals exist as positive ions in a 'sea' of delocalised electrons.

Metals are good electrical conductors because the delocalised electrons can move through the metal structure, i.e. an electrical current will flow through the metal.

Reactions of metals: redox reactions

The reactions of metals with oxygen, water and dilute acid can be used to work out an order of reactivity of metals known as the reactivity series.

Metals and oxygen

When metals react with oxygen the metal oxide is produced.

Magnesium reacts violently with oxygen to form magnesium oxide:

$$2Mg(s) + O_2(g) \rightarrow 2MgO(s)$$

Ionic equation: $2Mg(s) + O_2(g) \rightarrow 2Mg^{2+}O^{2-}(s)$

> **TOP TIP**
>
> Ion-electron equations are found in the SQA data booklet. Reductions are written as they are in the booklet, and oxidations are reversed.

Magnesium reacts violently with the oxygen in the air to form magnesium oxide.

The ionic equation shows the magnesium atoms have **lost electrons** and formed magnesium ions. Loss of electrons is called **oxidation**. The ion-electron equation for oxidation is written as:

$$Mg(s) \rightarrow Mg^{2+}(s) + 2e^- \quad \textbf{oxidation}$$

The oxygen has gained electrons from the magnesium so has been **reduced**:

$$O_2(g) + 4e^- \rightarrow 2O^{2-}(s) \quad \textbf{reduction}$$

Reduction and **ox**idation always happen together in a **redox** reaction.

The reduction and oxidation ion-electron equations can be added together in a redox equation. Electrons are not shown in a redox reaction because the electrons lost by the magnesium are gained by the oxygen, so they cancel out. The ion-electron equations are multiplied up to balance the electrons lost and gained:

Reduction: $O_2(g) + 4e^- \rightarrow 2O^{2-}(s)$

Oxidation: $2Mg(s) \rightarrow 2Mg^{2+}(s) + 4e^-$ (equation multiplied by 2 to balance the electrons)

Add to get

redox equation: $2Mg(s) + O_2(g) \rightarrow 2Mg^{2+}O^{2-}(s)$
(electrons cancel out)

> **TOP TIP**
>
> Ion-electron equations sometimes need to be multiplied to balance the electrons before adding to make the redox equation.

Metals and water

Sodium reacts violently with water to form sodium hydroxide.

Alkali metals (Group 1 in the periodic table) are so called because they react with water to give alkaline solutions.

When sodium reacts with water, sodium hydroxide and hydrogen gas are produced:

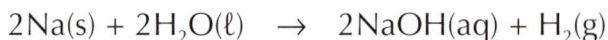

$$2Na(s) + 2H_2O(\ell) \rightarrow 2NaOH(aq) + H_2(g)$$

Ionic equation:

$$2Na(s) + 2H_2O(\ell) \rightarrow 2Na^+(aq) + 2OH^-(aq) + H_2(g)$$

The ionic equation shows the sodium has been oxidised and the water reduced:

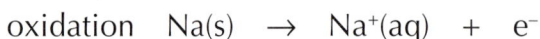

oxidation $Na(s) \rightarrow Na^+(aq) + e^-$

reduction $2H_2O(\ell) + 2e^- \rightarrow H_2(g) + 2OH^-(aq)$

redox $2Na(s) + 2H_2O(\ell) \rightarrow 2Na^+(aq) + 2OH^-(aq) + H_2(g)$

Metals and acids

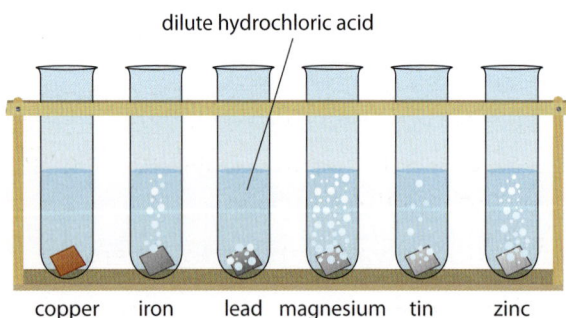

dilute hydrochloric acid

copper   iron   lead magnesium tin   zinc

Metals that react with an acid are oxidised.

When zinc reacts with dilute hydrochloric acid, zinc chloride and hydrogen are produced:

$$Zn(s) + 2HCl(aq) \rightarrow ZnCl_2(aq) + H_2(g)$$

Ionic equation: $Zn(s) + 2H^+(aq) + 2Cl^-(aq) \rightarrow Zn^{2+}(aq) + 2Cl^-(aq) + H_2(g)$

The ionic equation shows the zinc atoms have been oxidised and the hydrogen ions reduced:

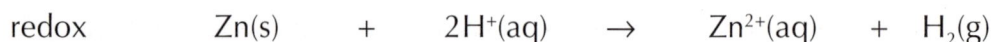

oxidation $Zn(s) \rightarrow Zn^{2+}(aq) + 2e^-$

reduction $2H^+(aq) + 2e^- \rightarrow H_2(g)$

redox $Zn(s) + 2H^+(aq) \rightarrow Zn^{2+}(aq) + H_2(g)$

Ion-electron and redox equations do not show ions that do not react (spectator ions). In this example the Cl^- ion is a spectator ion.

The reaction between metals and acids can be used to produce soluble salts. Excess metal is added to the acid, the mixture is fitered and the filtrate evaporated to dryness.

TOP TIP

You can remember the meaning of oxidation and reduction by the phrase 'OIL RIG'

Oxidation   Reduction
Is   Is
Loss of e⁻   Gain of e⁻

> ## Reactivity series
> Metals can be placed in order of reactivity by comparing the rates at which they react. This is known as the reactivity series:
>
> most reactive   least reactive
> K Na Li Ca Mg Al Zn Fe Sn Pb Cu Ag Au Pt

Quick Test

1. Copper metal is used in electrical flexes because it is a good conductor of electricity. Explain what makes metals good conductors of electricity.

2. Zinc reacts with oxygen to form zinc oxide:

   $$2Zn(s) + O_2(g) \rightarrow 2ZnO(s)$$

   (a) Write the ionic equation for the reaction.

   (b) Write the ion-electron equation for the oxidation of zinc.

   (c) Write the ion-electron equation for the reduction of oxygen.

   (d) Write the redox equation for the reaction.

3. When lithium reacts with water, lithium hydroxide and hydrogen gas are produced:

   $$2Li(s) + 2H_2O(\ell) \rightarrow 2LiOH(aq) + H_2(g)$$

   (a) Write the ionic equation for the reaction.

   (b) Write the ion-electron equation for the oxidation of lithium.

   (c) Write the ion-electron equation for the reduction of water.

   (d) Write the redox equation for the reaction.

4. When magnesium reacts with dilute sulfuric acid, magnesium sulfate and hydrogen are produced:

   $$Mg(s) + H_2SO_4(aq) \rightarrow MgSO_4(aq) + H_2(g)$$

   (a) Write the ionic equation for the reaction.

   (b) Write the ion-electron equation for the oxidation of magnesium.

   (c) Write the ion-electron equation for the reduction of the hydrogen ions.

   (d) Write the redox equation for the reaction.

Electrochemical cells

The electrochemical series

When different metals are connected and placed in an electrolyte (solution containing ions), an electric current flows. This is called an electrochemical cell. Comparing voltage readings between pairs of metals can be used to construct an electrochemical series. The electrochemical series can be used to predict the voltage and current direction in an electrochemical cell. The further apart the metals the higher the voltage. Electrons flow through connecting wires from the metal higher in the electrochemical series.

Cells involving metals

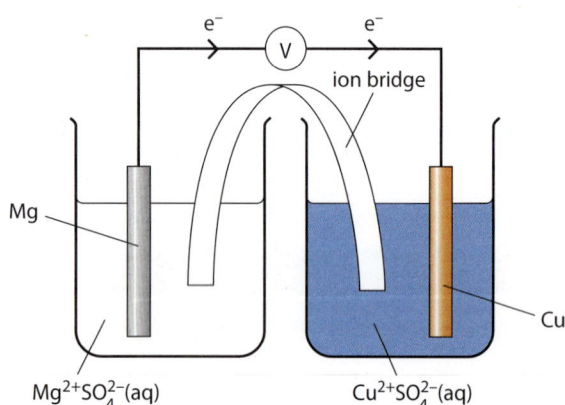

A chemical reaction takes place at each electrode in a chemical cell.

The **ion bridge** contains an electrolyte that allows ions to flow between the two solutions. Electrons flow from magnesium to copper, through the wire, because magnesium is higher than copper in the electrochemical series.

At the **magnesium electrode**: electrons flow from $Mg \rightarrow Cu$ (through the wire), so magnesium is **losing electrons** – magnesium atoms are being **oxidised** to magnesium ions. The ion-electron equation is:

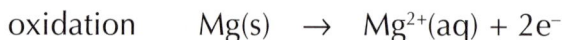

> oxidation $\quad Mg(s) \rightarrow Mg^{2+}(aq) + 2e^-$

At the **copper electrode**: the copper ions in the solution **gain electrons**, which have come from the magnesium. The copper ions are **reduced** to copper atoms. The ion-electron equation is:

> reduction $\quad Cu^{2+}(aq) + 2e^- \rightarrow Cu(s)$

Adding the reduction and oxidation equations gives the **redox** equation. Notice here that the electrons balance so there is no need to multiply either of the ion-electron equations. The spectator ion, ($SO_4^{2-}(aq)$), is not included.

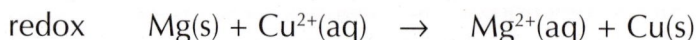

> redox $\quad Mg(s) + Cu^{2+}(aq) \rightarrow Mg^{2+}(aq) + Cu(s)$

TOP TIP

Read about reduction, oxidation and redox equations in **Properties and reactions of metals** before doing this section.

TOP TIP

The electrochemical series can be found in the SQA data booklet.

Cells involving non-metals

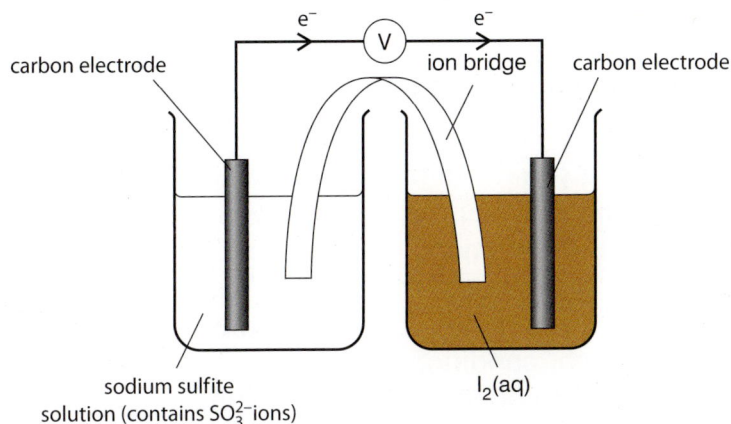

carbon electrode   ion bridge   carbon electrode

sodium sulfite solution (contains SO_3^{2-} ions) $I_2(aq)$

A chemical cell can be set up using non-metal electrodes. **Graphite** (a form of carbon) is often used because it conducts electricity and will not react with the electrolytes.

An example is the reaction between sodium sulfite and iodine:

The electrons flow from left to right. This is because at the left-hand electrode the sulfite ion is losing electrons – it is being **oxidised**:

oxidation $SO_3^{2-}(aq) + H_2O(\ell) \rightarrow SO_4^{2-}(aq) + 2H^+(aq) + 2e^-$

At the right-hand electrode the iodine molecule is gaining electrons – it is being **reduced**:

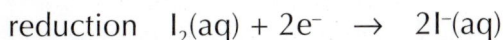

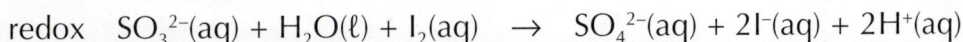

reduction $I_2(aq) + 2e^- \rightarrow 2I^-(aq)$

redox $SO_3^{2-}(aq) + H_2O(\ell) + I_2(aq) \rightarrow SO_4^{2-}(aq) + 2I^-(aq) + 2H^+(aq)$

Quick Test

1.   The diagram shows an electrochemical cell.

     (a) Write the ion-electron equation for the oxidation of zinc.

     (b) Write the ion-electron equation to show what happens to the silver ions at the silver electrode.

     (c) Name the process taking place at the silver electrode.

     (d) Add the ion-electron equations in (a) and (b) to give the redox equation.

     (e) In which direction do the electrons flow in the cell?

     (f) State the purpose of the ion bridge.

ion bridge

Zn   Ag

$Zn^{2+}SO_4^{2-}(aq)$ $Ag^+NO_3^-(aq)$

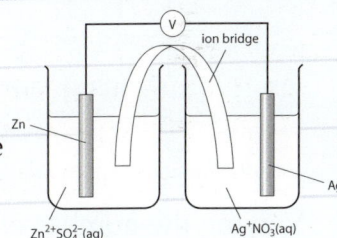

2.   The diagram shows an electrochemical cell. Electrons flow from left to right through the wire.

     (a) Write the ion-electron equation to show what happens to the iodide ion ($I^-(aq)$) at the left-hand electrode.

     (b) Name the process taking place at the left-hand electrode.

     (c) Write the ion-electron equation to show what happens to chlorine ($Cl_2(aq)$) at the right-hand electrode.

     (d) Name the process taking place at the right-hand electrode.

     (e) Add the ion-electron equations in (a) and (c) to give the redox equation.

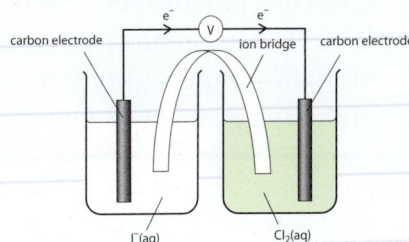

carbon electrode   ion bridge   carbon electrode

$I^-(aq)$ $Cl_2(aq)$

Plastics

Addition polymerisation

Polymers are giant molecules formed when lots of small molecules, known as monomers, join together. Plastics are common polymers.

The **poly(ethene)** used to make the playing surface of the London 2012 Olympic hockey pitch is an example of an <mark>addition polymer</mark>. Addition polymers are formed when lots of small **unsaturated** molecules (**monomers**) join together – in the case of poly(ethene) the monomer is **ethene**. The characteristic that makes hydrocarbon molecules like ethene suitable to undergo an addition reaction is the carbon-to-carbon **double bond (C=C)**. Under the right conditions the double bond breaks, resulting in electrons being made available to bond with neighbouring ethene molecules. Although the diagram shows only three molecules joining, in practice thousands of molecules join together.

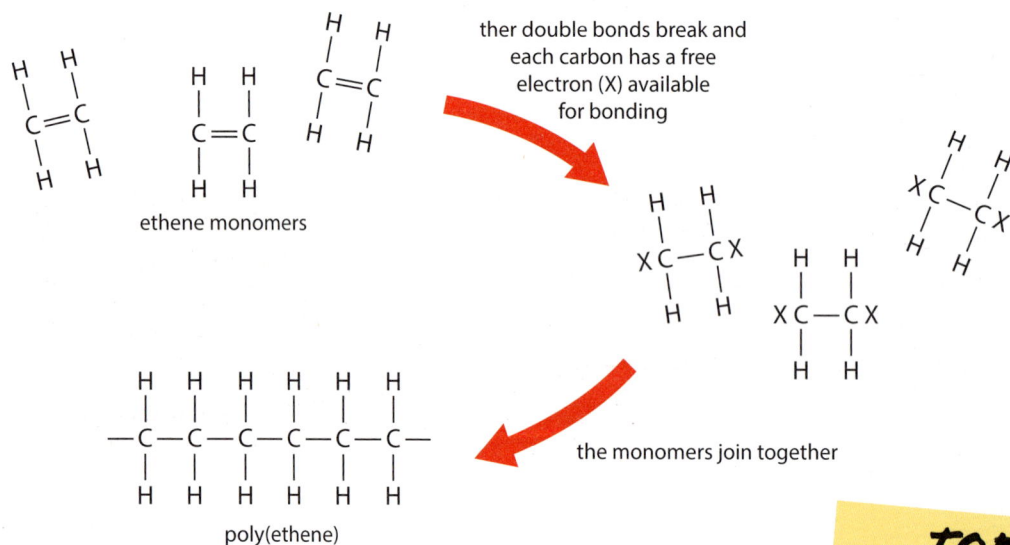

ther double bonds break and each carbon has a free electron (X) available for bonding

ethene monomers

the monomers join together

poly(ethene)

Lots of ethene molecules join to make poly(ethene).

Varying the number of carbon atoms in the polymer chain can change its properties. Poly(ethene) can be made soft and very flexible by keeping the chain lengths around 50 000 carbon atoms and having lots of branches. It can be made more rigid by making the chain length longer and having fewer branches.

TOP TIP

All addition polymers are made in the same way:
- The monomers must have a C=C double bond.
- The double bonds break.
- The monomers join to form a polymer.
- The name of the polymer comes from the name of the monomer, e.g. ethene → poly(thene).

Poly(propene) is another widely used addition polymer. It is very tough and flexible. As the name suggests, the monomer is propene. The diagram shows three propene monomers joining.

TOP TIP

Always draw the monomer in the I=I shape to make it easier to see how they join.

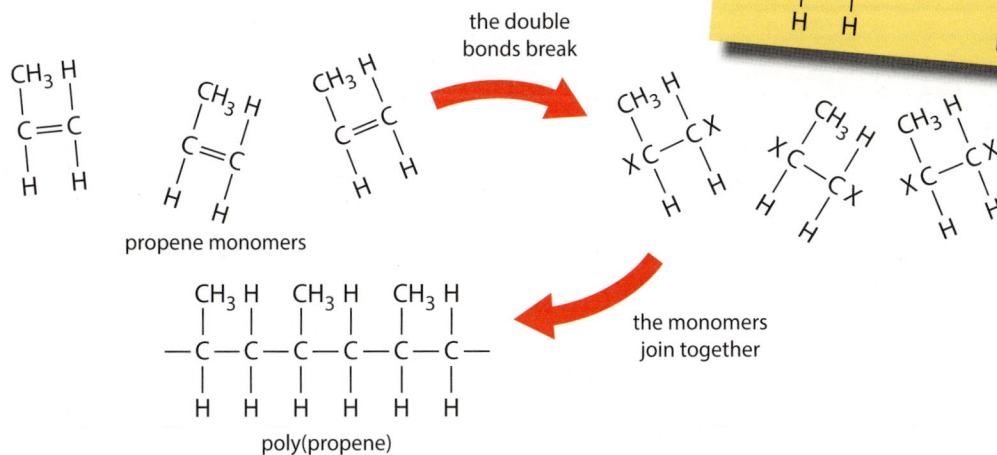

propene monomers

the double bonds break

the monomers join together

poly(propene)

The **repeating unit** in a polymer structure can be identified – it is shown in a bracket ([ ]).

TOP TIP

The repeating unit always has an open bond on each of the end carbon atoms.

Poly(propene)

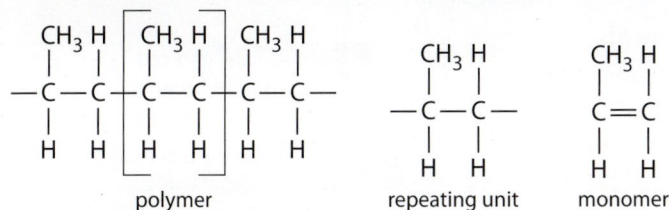

polymer   repeating unit   monomer

Quick Test

1. The monomer used to make polystyrene can be represented as:

    (a) Name the monomer.

    (b) Show how three of these monomer units join to form polystyrene.

    (c) Draw the repeating unit in polystyrene.

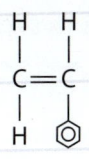

2. Part of the poly(tetrafluoroethene) molecule is shown:

    (a) Draw the repeating unit.

    (b) Draw the monomer unit.

    (c) Name the monomer.

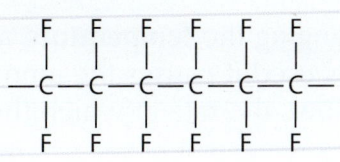

Ammonia – the Haber process

> ## Healthy plant growth
>
> Plants need nutrients in the form of the essential elements nitrogen (N), phosphorus (P) and potassium (K) for healthy growth. Synthetic fertilisers containing various percentages of N, P and K are made by chemists to help meet demand.

Making ammonia in the laboratory

Ammonia (NH_3) is the most important source of nitrogen, both on its own and in compounds.

Ammonia is a **gas** and can be made in the laboratory by heating an ammonium salt, such as ammonium chloride, with a base like solid calcium hydroxide or sodium hydroxide solution:

$$2NH_4Cl(s) \quad + \quad Ca(OH)_2(s) \quad \rightarrow \quad CaCl_2(s) \quad + \quad 2H_2O(l) \quad + \quad 2NH_3(g)$$

This way of making ammonia was one of the methods used before the Haber process was invented.

Ammonia is extremely **soluble** in water. This can be demonstrated in the fountain experiment. A dry flask filled with ammonia gas is inverted in a beaker of water.

Ammonia has a very strong smell, which can affect your breathing – it is the smell often associated with wet nappies.

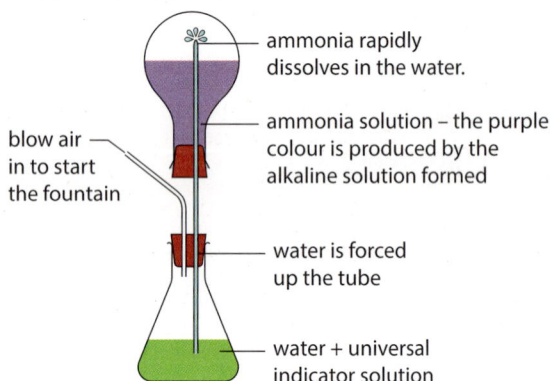

ammonia rapidly dissolves in the water.

ammonia solution – the purple colour is produced by the alkaline solution formed

blow air in to start the fountain

water is forced up the tube

water + universal indicator solution

The fountain experiment shows that ammonia is very soluble.

Industrial Production: the Haber process

Industrially, ammonia is made by the direct combination of nitrogen from the air and hydrogen obtained from natural gas.

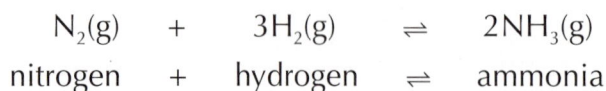

$$N_2(g) \quad + \quad 3H_2(g) \quad \rightleftharpoons \quad 2NH_3(g)$$

nitrogen   +   hydrogen $\rightleftharpoons$ ammonia

This is known as the Haber process, named after its inventor Fritz Haber.

It is well known that changing the **temperature** affects the rate of reactions, but if too high a temperature is used it causes the ammonia to break down. However, too low a temperature slows the rate at which the ammonia is formed.

Because the reactants and products are gases, increasing the **pressure** produces more ammonia.

The diagram summarises the Haber process:

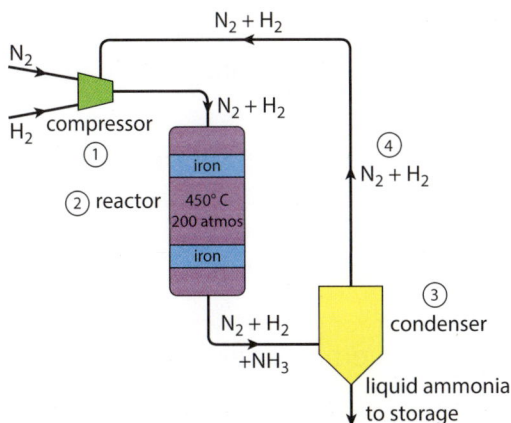

Simplified flow diagram for the manufacture of ammonia.

TOP TIP

The $\rightleftharpoons$ symbol indicates that the reaction is reversible, which means that as the nitrogen and hydrogen react to form ammonia, some of the ammonia breaks down and reforms the reactants, i.e. the reaction goes in a forward direction and a backward direction.

TOP TIP

Using a finely divided catalyst means there is a greater surface area for the reaction to take place on. The temperature is moderately high to make sure the ammonia is produced at an economical rate.

1. Nitrogen (from the air) and hydrogen (from natural gas) are compressed to a pressure of around **200 atmospheres** – 200 times higher than normal air pressure.

2. The compressed gases flow into the main reactor where they pass over a finely divided **iron catalyst** at about **450°C**.

3. The ammonia is passed into a condenser where it is cooled so that it **liquefies**.

4. Unreacted nitrogen and hydrogen are **recycled**. This saves valuable chemicals and helps push the yield of ammonia up to an economical amount (around 25%).

Quick Test

1. (a) Describe how ammonia gas could be made from ammonium sulfate.

    (b) How could you test the gas to show it was ammonia?

    (c) Suggest why any piece of equipment used to collect ammonia has to be dry.

2. Ammonia is produced industrially from its elements by the Haber process.

    (a) Write a balanced equation for the production of ammonia from its elements.

    (b) Summarise the conditions used in the Haber process.

    (c) Explain why there is such a low conversion rate of nitrogen and hydrogen to ammonia.

    (d) Explain why the temperature used in the process is not made lower.

    (e) Unreacted nitrogen and hydrogen are recycled. Why is this an important part of the process?

    (f) Explain why the catalyst is finely divided rather than being a solid piece of metal.

Nitric acid – the Ostwald process

Some of the **ammonia** produced by the Haber process is used to make **nitric acid** **(HNO$_3$)**.

It might seem more obvious to try to combine nitrogen and oxygen from the air to form nitrogen dioxide, which then dissolves in water to give nitric acid. Although it seems straightforward, the problem of nitrogen's lack of reactivity means that huge amounts of electricity are needed to supply the energy required to make the nitrogen react.

Wilhelm Ostwald invented the industrial method of converting ammonia into nitric acid, known as the **Ostwald process**.

He found that if ammonia and air were passed over a heated catalyst, nitrogen dioxide was formed, which dissolved in water to form nitric acid.

The diagram gives a simplified outline of the Ostwald process.

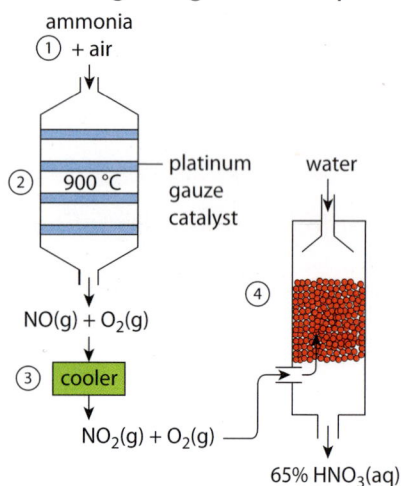

Simplified diagram showing the manufacture of nitric acid.

> **TOP TIP**
>
> The reaction between ammonia and oxygen in stage 2 is **exothermic**, so once the reaction has started, the external heating source can be reduced because the reaction produces its own energy. This saves a lot of energy so reduces costs.

Stage 1: A mixture of **ammonia** and **air** is compressed up to 14 atmospheres.

Stage 2: The ammonia/air mixture is passed through layers of **platinum gauze catalyst** at about **900°C** and **nitrogen oxide (NO)** is formed. The gauze provides a large surface area for the reaction to take place and allows the gases to move freely through it.

Stage 3: The nitrogen oxide and air are passed through a cooler where they react to form the brown gas **nitrogen dioxide (NO$_2$)**.

Stage 4: The nitrogen dioxide and air are passed up an absorption tower packed with small beads. Water falls freely over the beads and mixes with the nitrogen dioxide and air. Dilute **nitric acid (HNO$_3$)** is formed.

The equations for the reactions happening in stages 2–4 are:

Stage 2:

ammonia   +   oxygen   →   nitrogen monoxide   +   water

$4NH_3(g)$ + $5O_2(g)$ → $4NO(g)$ + $6H_2O(g)$

Stage 3:

nitrogen monoxide   +   oxygen   →   nitrogen dioxide

$2NO(g)$ + $O_2(g)$ → $2NO_2(g)$

Stage 4:

nitrogen dioxide   +   oxygen   +   water   →   nitric acid

$4NO_2(g)$ + $O_2(g)$ + $2H_2O(l)$ → $4HNO_3(aq)$

Ammonium nitrate

Most of the ammonia and nitric acid produced in the world is used to make **ammonium nitrate**, which is one of the most widely used **synthetic fertilisers**.

This is a **neutralisation** reaction:

ammonia   +   nitric acid   →   ammonium nitrate

$NH_3(g)$ + $HNO_3(aq)$ → $NH_4NO_3(aq)$

> **TOP TIP**
>
> Don't get confused between ammonia and ammonium. **Ammonia** is the gas made in the Haber process and has the formula NH_3. **Ammonium** is the ion with the formula NH_4^+. The ammonium ion is always part of a compound, e.g. ammonium nitrate.

Quick Test

1. The diagram shows a method for carrying out the Ostwald process in the laboratory.

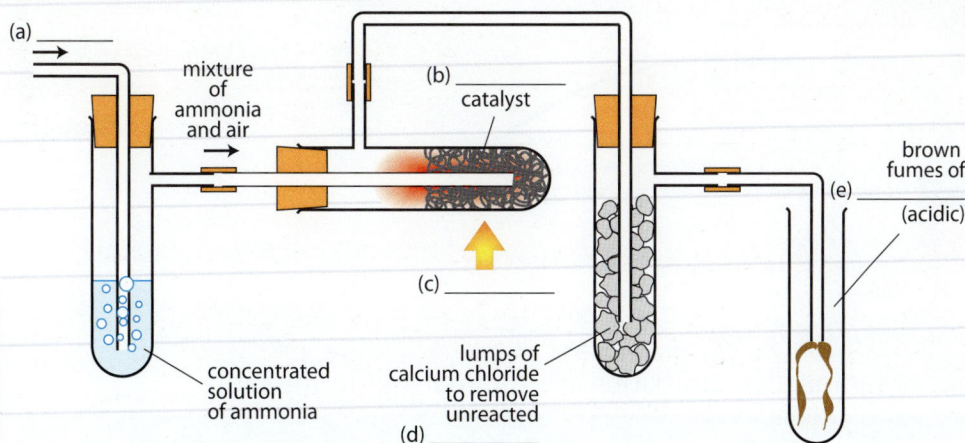

(a) Complete labels (a)–(e).

(b) How can the brown gas be tested to show that it is acidic?

(c) Why is it best to use platinum wire rather than a solid lump of platinum?

(d) Once the reaction has started the heat can be taken away.

Explain why this is the case.

(e) Describe the similarities and differences between the industrial Ostwald process and the laboratory process.

Radioactivity and radioisotopes

The atoms of most elements have **isotopes**. The nuclei of some of these isotopes are unstable and give out particles and rays, called **emissions**. This is known as **radioactivity**. Radioactivity happens spontaneously no matter what state the element is in or if it is chemically combined in a compound. These emissions are called **alpha (α)**, **beta (β)** and **gamma (γ)**.

The diagrams show the **penetrating power** of the radioactive emissions and what happens to them when they are passed through an **electric field**.

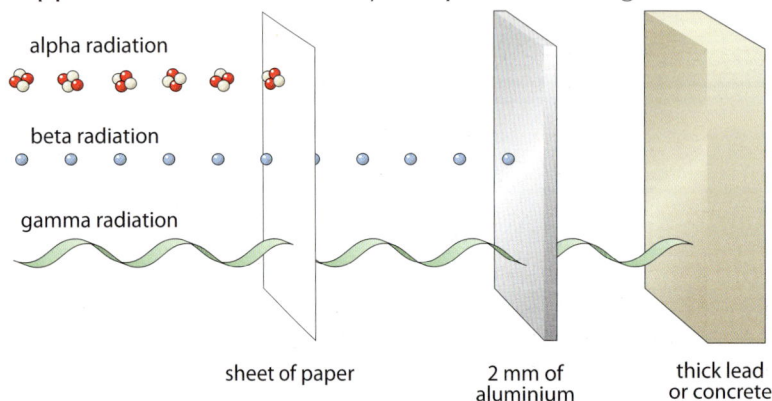

alpha radiation

beta radiation

gamma radiation

sheet of paper   2 mm of aluminium   thick lead or concrete

Penetrating power of radioactive emissions.

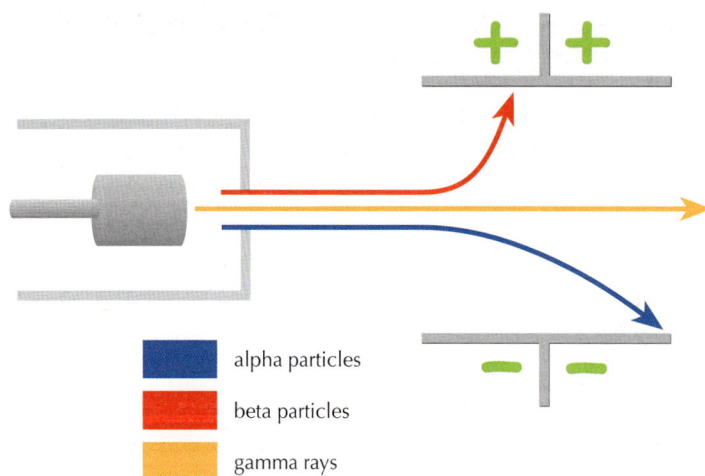

alpha particles

beta particles

gamma rays

Deflection of emissions in an electric field.

The properties of radioactive emissions are summarised in the table.

Name of emission	Distance travelled and penetrating power	Charge
Alpha (α)	Few centimetres in air. Stopped by paper.	positive
Beta (β)	Few metres in air. Stopped by thin aluminium sheet.	negative
Gamma (γ)	Miles in the air. Stopped by thick lead or concrete.	none

Properties of radioactive emissions

α **particles** are the heaviest of the emissions and are made up of two protons and two neutrons grouped together. An α particle is in fact a helium ion – He^{2+}. Its nuclide notation is $^4_2He^{2+}$ – the charge is often not shown.

β **particles** are high-energy electrons. A β particle is often represented as $^{\ 0}_{-1}e$.

γ **radiation** is not a particle and so has no mass and no charge. It is a **high-energy ray** that can travel long distances and has high penetration power.

Using radioactive isotopes

Radioactive isotopes are also known as **radioisotopes** and they are important in many everyday situations.

In the **home**: radioisotopes have limited use in the home but play a vital role in smoke alarms. They contain americium-241, which emits α particles that cause an electric current to flow. When smoke passes into the alarm's detector, the current drops and the alarm sounds.

In the **health service**: radioisotopes are used in a variety of ways. Cancer in the thyroid gland in the neck can be **detected** and **treated** using isotopes of iodine, which emit γ and β radiation.

In **industry**: radioisotopes are widely used to control the thickness of materials – this is known as **gauging**. The material passes between a radioactive source and a detector. The intensity of the radioactivity reduces when it hits the material. This is picked up by the detector, and the thickness of the material can be adjusted as necessary.

The fear of radioactivity damaging healthy cells and causing cancer is one of the main reasons for many people being concerned about the use of radioisotopes.

Quick Test

1. Complete the summary by filling in the missing words. You can use the word bank to help you.

Atoms with unstable (a)_____ can emit (b)_____ (α), beta (β) and (c)_____(γ) radiation. α particles are (d)_____ nuclei and β particles are high-energy (e)_____. α particles are (f)_____ moving and can be stopped by paper. (g)_____ particles are fast moving and can be stopped by a thin sheet of (h)_____ γ rays can travel long distances and can only be stopped by thick lead or concrete. Radioisotopes have many everyday uses. They are used in most (i)_____alarms in the home. In industry, (j)_____ the thickness of materials is controlled by radioisotopes. In the health service they are used in the detection and treatment of (k)_____. Radiation can (l)_____ healthy cells in the body as it passes through them.

Word bank

alpha, aluminium, beta, cancer, damage, electrons, gamma, gauging, helium, ionises, nuclei, slow, smoke

Nuclear equations and half-life

Nuclear equations

The breakdown of unstable nuclei (radiation) is also known as <mark>radioactive decay</mark>. An atom can decay through a series of stages until it forms atoms of a stable isotope.

The emission of an α particle means the nucleus of the original atom loses two protons and two neutrons. The emission of a β particle results in the original atom gaining a proton. γ radiation has no effect on the original atom because it is not a particle.

Radioactive decay can be represented by <mark>nuclear equations</mark> – they can be used to summarise the processes that produce α and β radiation.

Nuclear equations include the **mass number** (number of protons + neutrons), the **atomic number** (number of protons) and the **chemical symbol** for each particle involved, i.e. the nuclide notation.

Example of α **decay:**

When plutonium-242 decays by α ($^4_2$He) emission, uranium-238 is formed.

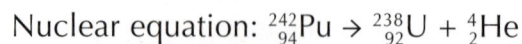

Nuclear equation: $^{242}_{94}$Pu $\rightarrow$ $^{238}_{92}$U + $^4_2$He

Example of β **decay:**

When thorium-234 decays by β ($^0_{-1}$e) emission, protactinium-234 is formed.

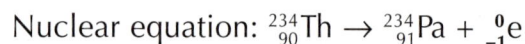

Nuclear equation: $^{234}_{90}$Th $\rightarrow$ $^{234}_{91}$Pa + $^0_{-1}$e

> ### TOP TIP
> The total of the mass number on the left of the arrow must equal the total on the right of the arrow. It is the same for the atomic numbers. Atomic numbers are in the SQA data booklet.

Note again that when the mass numbers and atomic numbers are added on each side of the arrow they are the same. The electron (β particle) is given an unusual atomic number (−1). This is a way of indicating that an extra proton is gained by the parent atom when a beta particle is emitted and so the rule that the total atomic number must be the same on each side of the arrow is satisfied.

So long as you know the particle being emitted, the element formed can be worked out, as illustrated in the following examples.

Example 1: Work out what a, b and X are in the nuclear equation:

$^{220}_{86}$Rn $\rightarrow$ ^a_bX + $^4_2$He

Worked answer: Apply the rule that mass and atomic numbers must add up to the same on each side of the equation.

So, a = 216; b = 84 so X must be Po (polonium), i.e. $^{216}_{84}$Po

Example 2: Work out what c, d and Z are in the nuclear equation:

$^{228}_{88}$Ra $\rightarrow$ ^c_dZ + $^0_{-1}$e

Worked answer: Apply the rule that mass and atomic numbers must add up to the same on each side of the equation.

So, c = 228; d = 89 so Z must be Ac (actinium), i.e. $^{228}_{89}\text{Ac}$

Artificial radioisotopes can be made in nuclear reactors by bombarding stable nuclei with neutrons. For example:

$$^{27}_{13}\text{Al} + ^{1}_{0}\text{n} \rightarrow ^{24}_{11}\text{Na} + ^{4}_{2}\text{He}$$

The sodium isotope produced is radioactive and decays itself by β emission:

$$^{24}_{11}\text{Na} \rightarrow ^{24}_{12}\text{Mg} + ^{0}_{-1}\text{e}$$

Radioactive phosphorus-32 is produced by neutron bombardment of sulfur-32. A proton ($^{1}_{1}\text{p}$) is also produced:

$$^{32}_{16}\text{S} + ^{1}_{0}\text{n} \rightarrow ^{32}_{15}\text{P} + ^{1}_{1}\text{p}$$

Many artificial radioisotopes are produced for specific uses in health care and industry.

> ***TOP TIP***
>
> Learn the notation for particles: neutron: $^{1}_{0}\text{n}$; proton: $^{1}_{1}\text{p}$; β (electron): $^{0}_{-1}\text{e}$; α: $^{4}_{2}\text{He}$.

Half-life

The nuclei of radioisotopes decay in a random fashion. The time in which half of the nuclei of a radioisotope would be expected to decay is known as the **half-life**, often abbreviated to $t_{1/2}$. Each radioisotope has a unique half-life and this can vary from fractions of a second to millions of years. The half-life is constant, unaffected by chemical or physical conditions.

Radioisotope	Half-life	Use
Iodine-131	8.02 days	Diagnosing/treating diseases associated with the thyroid gland
Technetium-99m	6.01 hours	Imaging the organs of the body
Americium-241	433 years	Smoke detectors
Caesium-137	30.07 years	Thickness gauging

Selection of radioisotope half-lives

Radioactive isotopes with short half-lives are used for medical diagnoses and treatment, because radioactivity can damage healthy cells in the body.

As the atoms of a radioisotope decay, the intensity of the radiation decreases. After one half-life the intensity of the radiation will have fallen to half its original value. After a second half-life the intensity of the radiation will have halved again, i.e. it will be one quarter of its original value. A graph of the intensity of the radiation emitted against time gives a radioactive **decay curve** with a typical shape.

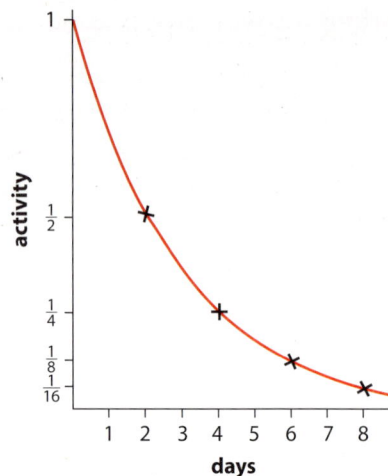

Decay curve for a radioisotope with a half-life of two days.

The graph shows the change in activity for a radioisotope where $t_{1/2}$ = two days.

The graph shows it takes two days (one half-life) for the intensity of the radiation to halve. After two half-lives (four days) the intensity of the radiation will have dropped to a quarter of its original value and so on.

So, if you start with 1 g of the sample, after one half-life (two days) half of the original sample (0.5 g) will have decayed, leaving the other 0.5 g active. After another half-life (four days total) half of the remaining 0.5 g will decay, leaving 0.25 g of the original sample. After a third half-life (six days) half of the 0.25 g will have decayed, leaving 0.125 g of the original sample. So, after three half-lives only 0.125 g of the original sample will be left.

Worked example: Sodium-24 has a half-life of 15 hours. What mass of a 0.4 g sample of sodium-24 would be left after 60 hours?

Answer: Number of half-lives = 60/15 = $4t_{1/2}$

After $1t_{1/2}$ (15 hours), 0.2 g left

After $2t_{1/2}$ (30 hours), 0.1 g left

After $3t_{1/2}$ (45 hours), 0.05 g left

After $4t_{1/2}$ (60 hours), 0.025 g left.

Dating using radioisotopes

To work out the age of material, researchers compare the ratio of a radioactive isotope of an element present in a sample with the proportion of stable isotope present and compare the ratio with a sample of the same material at the present time. By doing this and knowing the half-life of the radioisotope they can calculate how much time has passed.

Radiocarbon dating

Carbon dating is one of the most widely known uses of radioisotopes. It is used in archaeological research and can be used to date specimens containing material that was once living.

Potassium-argon dating

Radiocarbon dating is only useful for materials less than about 50 000 years old owing to the very small amount of ^{14}C present in materials older than this.

Other methods making use of radioisotopes with much longer half-lives have to be used to date rocks and fossils.

One system that has been very successful in dating the ages of fossils is ==potassium–argon dating==. Potassium is an extremely common element. Although most potassium isotopes aren't radioactive, one of them is, and one of its decay products is the gas argon.

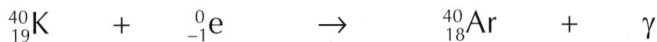

$$^{40}_{19}K \quad + \quad ^{0}_{-1}e \quad \rightarrow \quad ^{40}_{18}Ar \quad + \quad \gamma$$

The half-life for this transition is 1.3 billion years.

Quick Test

1. Write nuclear equations for the following:

   (a) The α decay of $^{234}_{92}U$.

   (b) The β decay of $^{228}_{89}Ac$.

   (c) The decay of ^{210}Bi to ^{210}Po.

   (d) The neutron bombardment of $^{45}_{21}Sc$, which produces $^{42}_{19}K$ and an α particle.

2. The decay curve for strontium-90 is shown:

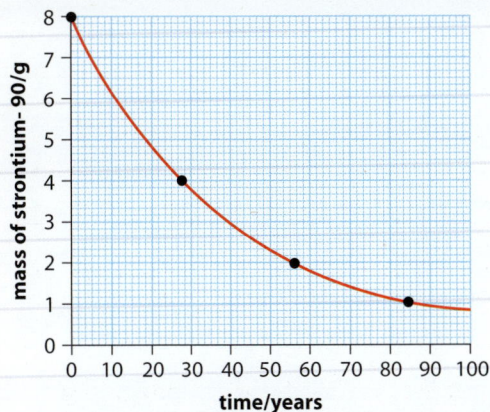

   (a) Use the graph to work out the half-life of strontium-90.

   (b) How long would it take for the mass of the strontium-90 to fall to 2.5 g?

   (c) What mass of strontium-90 would be left after $t_{1/2} = 3$?

3. Give **one** example of how radioisotopes are used:

   (a) at home

   (b) in industry

   (c) in medicine

Chemical apparatus and techniques

Apparatus

You should be familiar with and know how and when to use the pieces of apparatus listed in the table.

- Beaker
- Burette
- Conical flask
- Delivery tubes
- Dropper
- Evaporating basin
- Filter funnel
- Measuring cylinder
- Pipette and safety filler
- Test tube/boiling tube
- Thermometer

Techniques

You be familiar with the following techniques and be able to draw labelled, sectional diagrams for common apparatus.

Filtration

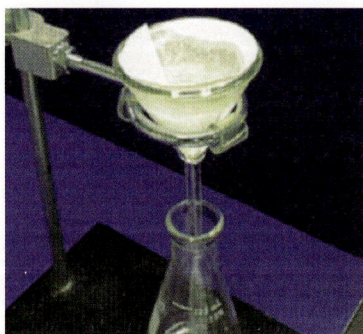

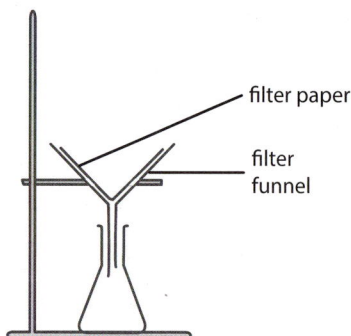

Filtration set up in the laboratory and labelled sectional diagram.

Using a balance

A balance allows you to accurately weigh the mass of a substance. Typical school balances will measure masses, in grams, correct to one or two decimal places. More accurate balances used for analytical work will measure to four decimal places.

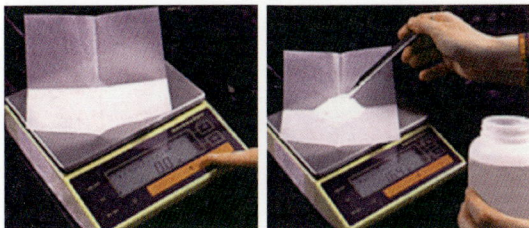

Measuring the mass of a substance using a top pan balance.

Collecting gases

The sectional diagrams show common methods of gas collection. The method depends on the solubility of the gas and how pure a sample is required.

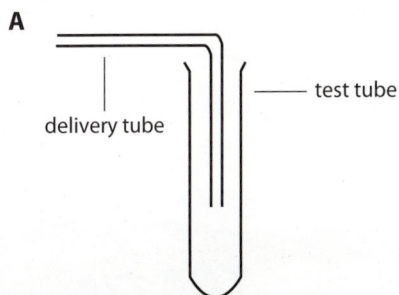

A

test tube

delivery tube

Upward displacement of air for soluble gases which are more dense than air

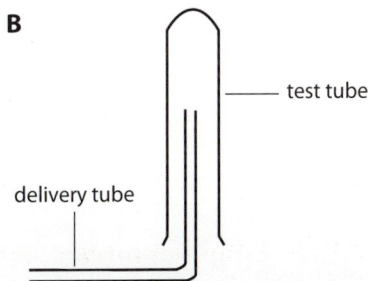

B

test tube

delivery tube

Downward displacement of air for soluble gases which are less dense than air

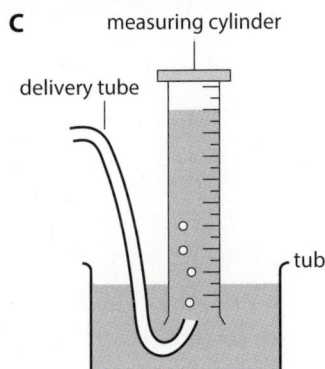

C

measuring cylinder

delivery tube

tub

Collection over water for relatively insoluble gases

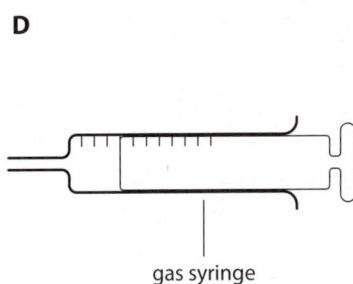

D

gas syringe

A gas syringe can be used to collect a pure sample of any gas

Sectional diagrams showing the different methods of collecting a gas.

Heating methods

The two most common heating methods used in school laboratories are using a Bunsen burner or electric hot plate. A Bunsen burner can reach very high temperatures. For safety reasons it should not be used for heating flammable substances like alcohol. A hot plate is used when lower temperatures are required and can be used with flammable liquids like alcohol as there is no naked flame.

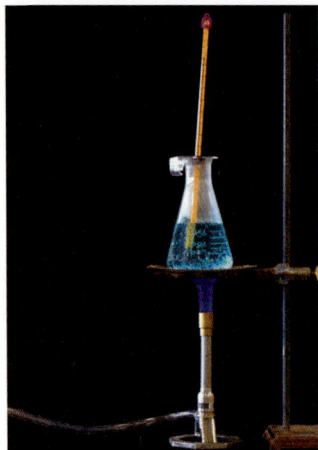

A Bunsen burner can heat substances to a high temperature.

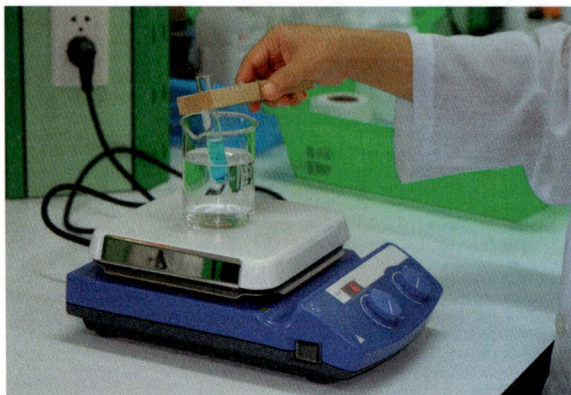

A hot plate can be safely used to heat flammable liquids.

Preparation of soluble salts

1 Acids with metals (see page 72).

2 Acids with bases – metal oxides, metal hydroxides and metal carbonates (see page 40).

Preparation of insoluble salts

Dissolve soluble compounds containing the ions required in the insoluble salt, in separate beakers.

Mix the solutions – a precipitate (the insoluble salt) will be produced.

Filter and wash the precipitate and allow it to dry.

> **TOP TIP**
>
> A solubility table can be found in the SQA data booklet.

Testing electrical conductivity

A circuit diagram showing a simple conductivity tester for solid substances is shown. If the bulb lights when the substance is placed in the circuit then it is an electrical conductor. Solutions and liquids can be tested in the same way using carbon electrodes which are placed into the solution or liquid.

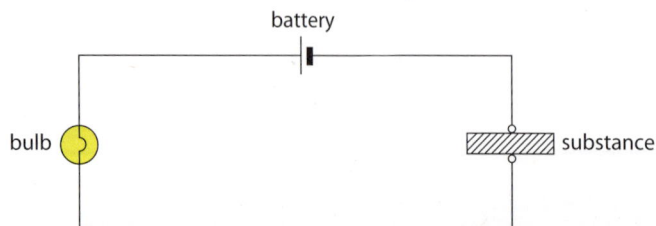

Setting up an electrochemical cell

In an electrochemical cell metal or carbon electrodes are placed in an electrolyte (ionic solution) and connected by a wire. The electrolytes and electrodes can be in separate beakers connected by a salt bridge (see pages 74/75).

Electrolysis of solutions

Electrolysis is the breaking down of a compound by passing electricity through it. A direct current (d.c.) has to be used in order to identify the products. In a direct current one side is negative the other positive. Positive ions are attracted to the negative electrode and negative ions are attracted to the positive electrode. The diagram shows the electrolysis of copper(II) chloride solution.

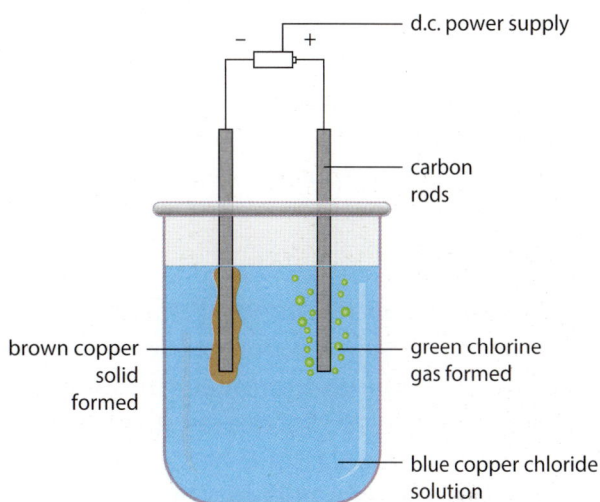

d.c. power supply

carbon rods

brown copper solid formed

green chlorine gas formed

blue copper chloride solution

Determination of E_h

The amount of energy given (E_h) out during a chemical reaction out can be calculated indirectly from experimental results (see page 64)

Reporting experimental work

You should include the following, where appropriate, when writing a report about an experiment.

- Labelled sectional diagrams of common chemical apparatus.
- Tables of data with appropriate headings and units.
- Present data as a bar, line or scatter graph with suitable scales and labels.
- Draw a line of best fit to represent a trend observed in experimental data.
- Calculate an average (mean) from data.
- Suggest and justify an improvement to an experimental method.

Qualitative analysis

Laboratory qualitative analysis techniques

Detecting substances that are present in our environment is known as **qualitative analysis**. The techniques used nowadays are fairly sophisticated but their origins can be traced back to simple laboratory experiments. Flame testing, precipitation reactions and chromatography are all examples of qualitative analysis techniques used in the laboratory.

Flame testing

When some metal compounds are placed in a flame, characteristic colours are observed. For instance when **sodium** compounds are placed in a flame a **yellow** colour is observed. **Potassium** gives a **lilac** flame. When the metal compounds are heated some electrons of the metal ions gain energy. The flame colours arise when the electrons lose the energy again. The energy is emitted as light of a certain colour, which is different for each metal.

A flame test.

Precipitation

Some **metal ions** can also be detected using **precipitation** reactions. When two solutions are mixed, and a solid forms, it is called a precipitate.

When **sodium hydroxide** solution is added to solutions containing metal ions **coloured** precipitates can be formed. If the solution contains iron(III) ions a rust-red precipitate of iron(III) hydroxide is formed.

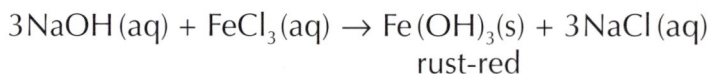

TOP TIP

Flame colours and solubility tables can be found in the SQA data booklet.

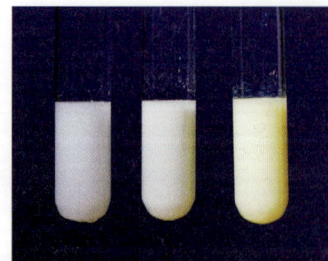

$$3NaOH(aq) + FeCl_3(aq) \rightarrow Fe(OH)_3(s) + 3NaCl(aq)$$
$$\text{rust-red}$$

The colour of the precipitate helps identify the metal ion present.

Non-metal ions can also be detected using precipitation reactions.

When **silver nitrate** is added to solutions containing halide (group 7) ions, precipitates form. The **colour** of the precipitate indicates the particular halide ion present. When silver nitrate is added to a sodium **chloride** solution a white precipitate of silver chloride is obtained.

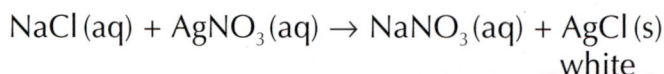

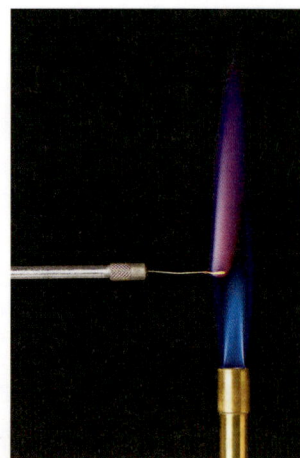

$$NaCl(aq) + AgNO_3(aq) \rightarrow NaNO_3(aq) + AgCl(s)$$
$$\text{white}$$

Precipitation reactions.

Testing for gases

Oxygen

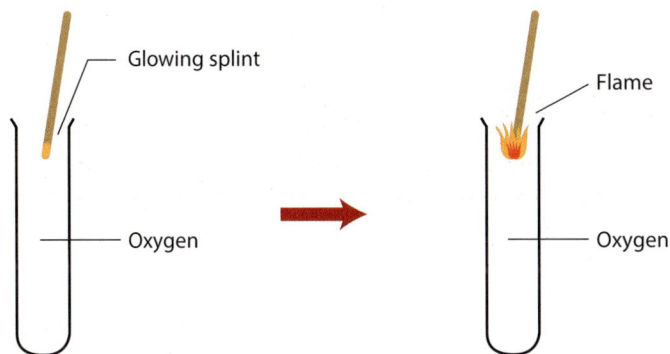

Glowing splint put in oxygen   Oxygen ignites a glowing splint

Hydrogen   **Carbon dioxide**

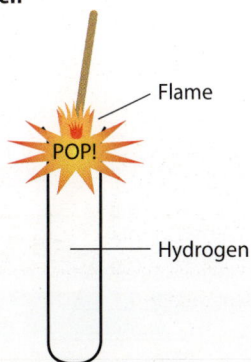

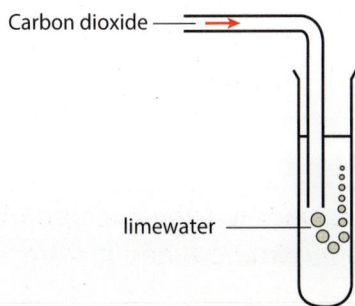

Hydrogen burns with a 'pop'   Carbon dioxide turns limewater cloudy

Quick Test

1. You are given soil samples from the Moon and asked to analyse them to find out if certain elements are present. Describe how you would test for:

    (a) potassium

    (b) iron(III) ions

    (c) halide ions.

Quantitative analysis

Titration

Chemists are interested in which substances are present but also how much of these substances are present. This is **quantitative analysis**. One method used to work out how much of a substance is present in a solution is **titration**. Titration can be used to find the concentration of an acid or alkali using a neutralisation reaction.

How to do a titration

The concentration of a sodium hydroxide solution, say, can be found by titrating the solution with a dilute acid such as hydrochloric acid.

Step 1: A **pipette** is used to transfer a known quantity of the sodium hydroxide solution into a conical flask.

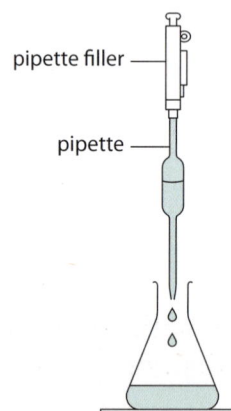

pipette filler

pipette

Step 2: Two or three drops of a suitable **indicator** are added to the solution and the flask placed on a white tile.

Step 3: A **burette** is filled with acid of an accurately known concentration (standard solution).

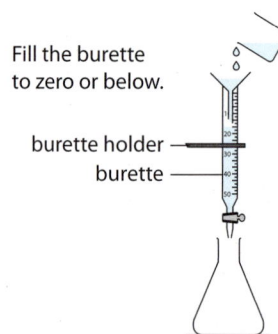

Fill the burette to zero or below.

burette holder

burette

Step 4: Add the acid to the sodium hydroxide solution in the flask until there is a **colour change** (purple to lime green) and note the volume on the burette. This is often called the **end-point**.

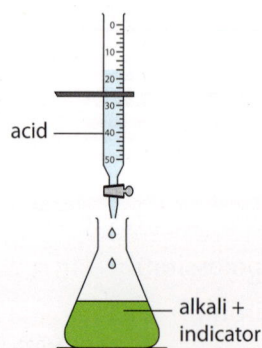

acid

alkali + indicator

Accuracy counts

When titration is used in quantitative analysis, a rough titration to estimate the volume of solution that needs to be added is carried out. The titration is then carried out accurately to find the exact volume that needs to be added. It is good practice to repeat the titration until ==concordant titres== are obtained. Concordant titres are where the volumes titrated are within 0.2 cm^3. The values are averaged (ignoring the rough titration) for use in the titration calculation.

$$\text{Average} = \frac{12.1+11.9}{2}$$
$$= 12.0 \text{ cm}^3$$

Titration	1st level (cm^3)	2nd level (cm^3)	Volume added (cm^3)
1st (rough)	0.0	12.9	12.9
2nd	12.9	25.0	12.1
3rd	25.0	36.9	11.9

In this example 12.1 cm^3 and 11.9 cm^3 are averaged because they are concordant values.

Using titration

Titration is used widely in industry. In wineries, for example, it is used to check the acidity of the wine, as this affects the keeping quality of the wine. In the dairy industry, titration is part of a procedure that measures the protein content of foods.

Titration allows the concentration of dissolved oxygen in water to be worked out. This is important in order to monitor the quality of water in lochs and rivers. Fish can't survive without good water quality.

The water quality in many of Scotland's rivers has improved over recent years. Salmon are now being caught on the River Clyde after an absence from the river of many years. The Clyde suffered badly from industrial pollution.

Quick Test

1. (a) Describe how to carry out a titration with an acid and alkali.
   (b) The results of three titrations are shown:

Titration	1st level (cm^3)	2nd level (cm^3)	Volume of sodium hydroxide added (cm^3)
1st	0.2	15.6	15.4
2nd	15.4	30.3	14.9
3rd	30.3	45.0	14.7

Work out the average volume of sodium hydroxide used to neutralise the acid.

2. Give two examples of how titrations are used in chemical analysis in everyday life.

Learning checklist

In this chapter you have learned:

Metals from ores

- the percentage composition by mass of a metal in an ore can be calculated
- metals can be extracted from their ores by heating, smelting and electrical methods, depending on their reactivity
- extraction of a metal from its ore is called reduction
- reduction of ores involves metal ions gaining electrons
- the reducing agent can be identified in a reaction

Properties and reactions of metals

- in metals the outer electrons are delocalised
- metallic bonding involves the attraction of metal ions for delocalised outer electrons of neighbouring atoms
- the properties of metals including electrical conductivity are explained by metallic bonding
- oxidation is the opposite of reduction and involves the loss of electrons by a reactant
- reduction and oxidation always take place together
- the combined reduction and oxidation reaction is called a redox reaction
- ion-electron equations can be written to describe the processes of reduction and oxidation
- ion-electron equations are found in the SQA data booklet
- redox equations can be formed by combining the ion-electron equations for reduction and oxidation
- the reactions of metals with water, oxygen and acids are examples of redox reactions and can be described using ionic equations and redox equations

Electrochemical cells

- the reactions in electrochemical cells are examples of redox reactions
- the reactions at the electrodes in electrochemical cells can be described using ion-electron equations
- ion-electron equations for the reactions at the electrodes can be combined to give a redox equation for the cell reaction

Addition polymerisation

- how three ethene molecules join to make part of a poly(ethene) molecule
- monomers for making addition polymers must have a C=C double bond
- the structure of an addition polymer can be drawn from the structure of its monomer
- the structure of the repeating unit and the monomer can be drawn from the structure of an addition polymer
- an addition polymer can be recognised from its carbon backbone

Ammonia – the Haber process

- ammonia is an important feedstock for the manufacture of fertilisers
- ammonia can be made in the laboratory by heating an ammonium salt with a base
- ammonia is very soluble and forms an alkaline solution when it dissolves in water
- ammonia is made industrially by the Haber process
- in the Haber process nitrogen from the air combines with hydrogen from the petrochemical industry
- the reaction of nitrogen with hydrogen to make ammonia is reversible, and the ammonia breaks down if the temperature is too high
- the Haber process needs a temperature of 450°C, a pressure of 200 atmospheres and an iron catalyst

Nitric acid – the Ostwald process

- nitric acid is an important feedstock for the manufacture of ammonium nitrate
- nitric acid is made industrially by the Ostwald process
- in the Ostwald process ammonia and oxygen are passed over a platinum catalyst at 900°C
- the reaction is exothermic so external heat can be removed when the reaction gets started
- nitrogen monoxide is initially formed, then nitrogen dioxide, which is dissolved in water
- nitrogen dioxide is made in the air during lightning storms
- ammonium nitrate is formed when ammonia and nitric acid react in a neutralisation reaction
- ammonium nitrate is used as a fertiliser

Radioactivity and radioisotopes

- there are many unstable isotopes of elements
- unstable isotopes can become more stable by emitting radiation
- isotopes that emit radiation are known as radioactive isotopes or radioisotopes
- radioisotopes have many important industrial and medical uses
- the three types of radiation emitted from nuclei are alpha (α), beta (β) and gamma (γ)
- alpha and beta radiation changes an isotope of one element to an isotope of another element
- alpha particles are helium nuclei ($_2^4\text{He}^{2+}$), i.e they are heavy positively charged particles
- alpha particles are slow moving and have low penetration – they will only travel a few centimetres through air
- beta particles are electrons and are fast moving, i.e. they are negatively charged
- a beta particle is emitted when a neutron changes to a proton in the nucleus
- beta particles are more penetrating than alpha particles but are stopped by a thin sheet of aluminium
- gamma radiation is produced by nuclei losing energy

Nuclear equations and half-life

- nuclear equations are used to describe the transitions that produce radiations
- the mass numbers and atomic numbers of isotopes are shown in nuclear equations
- the time in which half of the nuclei of a radioisotope decay is known as the half-life
- half-lives for radioisotopes are unique and constant
- the age of materials can be dated using the half-lives of radioisotopes

Qualitative analysis

- qualitative analysis is the name given to the group of techniques that indicate which substances are present
- qualitative analysis techniques include flame testing, precipitation and testing for oxygen, hydrogen and carbon dioxide

Quantitative analysis

- quantitative analysis allows the amount of a substance present to be calculated
- titration is a quantitative analysis method that is widely used in industry

Glossary

addition polymer: formed when lots of small unsaturated molecules (monomers) join together

addition reaction: one of the bonds of the carbon-to-carbon double bond is broken and new atoms (or groups) join to the carbon chain

alcohols: a homologous series containing the hydroxyl functional group (–O-H)

alpha (α) particles: a helium ion ($^4_2\text{He}^{2+}$) – one of the radioactive emissions given out by unstable nuclei

ammonia: the gas made in the Haber process and has the formula NH_3

ammonium: the ion with the formula NH_4^+. The ammonium ion is always part of a compound, e.g. ammonium nitrate

angular: bent shape three atoms joined in a molecule can take up eg H_2O

atom: what everything is made from

atomic number: number of protons in an atom

average rate: the change in the quantity of reactant or product over time

balanced equation: the total number of atoms of each element on the left-hand side of the equation equals the total on the right

beta (β) particles: a high-energy electron ($^0_{-1}\text{e}$) – one of the radioactive emissions given out by unstable nuclei

branched chain: a hydrocarbon structure consisting of carbon atoms covalently bonded to each other with a side group attached, e.g. methyl (–CH_3)

burette: graduated glass tube with a tap at one end used to deliver variable volumes of a solution in titrations

carbon dating: method that uses the amount of unstable carbon-14 (^{14}C) present in a once–living material to calculate its age

carboxyl group:

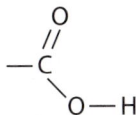

carboxylic acids: acids containing the carboxyl functional group

combustion: the reaction of a fuel with oxygen producing energy (exothermic)

concentration: a measure of the quantity of a substance (mass or moles) dissolved in a specific volume of water (litres): $C = m / V$ or $C = n / V$

concordant titres: titrations are carried out until the volumes measured at the point where the reaction is complete are very close to each other. The values are averaged (ignoring the rough titration)

covalent network: a giant three-dimensional structure in which all the atoms are covalently bonded to each other

cycloalkanes: a homologous series of saturated hydrocarbon with the carbons arranged in a ring

decay curve: a graph of the intensity of the radiation emitted against time

dehydration: the removal of water from a molecule, e.g. alcohol → alkene

delocalised electrons: electrons that can move easily from one atom to another

direct current (dc): gives a positive and negative electrode so products of electrolysis can be identified

dissociation of water: a small proportion of water molecules break down into equal concentrations of hydrogen ions and hydroxide ions

dot and cross diagram: dots and crosses are used to represent electrons in diagrams showing how atoms bond

Glossary

electrolysis: breaking down an ionic compound by passing a dc current through it

electron (e⁻): negatively charged particle which moves around the nucleus of an atom

electrostatic forces: attraction between oppositely charged ions

element: substance made from the same atoms

emissions: particles and rays given out by unstable nuclei

endothermic: energy is taken in from the surroundings during a chemical reaction

end-point: point in a titration where the indicator changes colour often at the point of neutralisation

exothermic: a reaction in which energy is given out

finite: will not last for ever

functional group: an atom or group of atoms (including the C$=$C double bond) within molecules in a homologous series that gives them particular properties

gamma (γ) rays: high-energy radiation – one of the radioactive emissions given out by unstable nuclei

general formula: the formulae of compounds in a homologous series follow a pattern, which can be represented by a general formula, e.g. alkanes C_nH_{2n+2} where n = 1, 2, 3, etc.

gram formula mass (GFM): the formula mass of a compound measured in grams

graphite: a form of carbon often used as electrodes in an electrochemical cell because it conducts electricity and will not react with the electrolytes

group: vertical column in the periodic table

group ions: ions with more than one atom, e.g. sulfate (SO_4^{2-})

Haber process: industrial preparation of ammonia

half-life (t$_{1/2}$): the time in which half of the nuclei of a radioisotope would be expected to decay

homologous series: a family of compounds that have similar chemical properties and show a gradual change in physical properties, e.g. boiling point, and can be represented by the same general formula

hydration: an addition reaction that involves adding water across a double carbon-to-carbon bond to form an alcohol

hydrogenation: an addition reaction where hydrogen adds on to a molecule across the double carbon-to-carbon bond in an alkene (unsaturated) giving the corresponding alkane (saturated)

hydroxyl group: –O-H

indicator: a chemical that changes colour at the point where a reaction is complete

ion bridge: an electrolyte that allows ions to flow between the two solutions in an electrochemical cell

ion-electron equation: equations that show the electrons gained or lost by an atom or ion. The SQA data booklet gives a list of commonly used ion-electron equations

ionic lattice: a giant structure with oppositely charged positive (metal) ions and negative (non-metal) ions

isomers: molecules with the same molecular formula but different structural formula

isotopes: atoms with the same atomic number but different mass numbers

linear: atoms joined in a straight line

mass number: the number of protons and neutrons in an atom added together

mole: the gram formula mass of a substance

molecule: grouping of non-metal atoms joined by covalent bonds

neutralisation: when an acid reacts with a base to form water

neutron (n): neutral particle in the nucleus of most atoms

nuclear equations: a shorthand way of representing radioactive decay, e.g.
$^{242}_{94}Pu \rightarrow \, ^{238}_{92}U + \, ^{4}_{2}He$

nuclide notation: a shorthand way of showing the mass number and atomic number of an atom along with the symbol of the element

ores: rocks from which metals can be obtained

Ostwald process: industrial manufacture of nitric acid

oxidation: loss of electrons

pipette: glass tube used to transfer a known volume of solution

proton (p): positively charged particle in the nucleus of an atom

qualitative analysis: detecting chemicals that are present in a substance

quantitative analysis: detecting how much of a chemical is present in a substance

radioactive decay: name given to the process when unstable nuclei break down

radioactivity: emissions given out by unstable nuclei

radioisotopes: another name for a radioactive isotope

redox equation: reduction and oxidation ion-electron equations added together

redox reaction: reaction in which loss and gain of electrons take place

relative atomic mass (RAM): average of the masses of the isotopes of an element

repeating unit: part of the structure of a polymer that repeats the length of the structure

reversible reaction: a reaction in which products break down to form reactants as they form, often represented by the $\rightleftharpoons$ symbol

reduction: gain of electrons

reducing agent: substance that brings about reduction, i.e. supplies electrons

shared pair of electrons: when two electrons from two atoms are shared, a covalent bond is formed

smelting: reducing a metal ore by heating with carbon

spectator ions: ions that do not take part in a reaction

straight chain: a hydrocarbon structure consisting of carbon atoms covalently bonded to each other with no branches (side chains)

systematic naming: an internationally agreed method of naming compounds that is used throughout the world

tetrahedral: the shape a molecule with five atoms can take up eg CH_4

titration: method of carrying out a chemical reaction by adding accurate quantities of reactants to work out the unknown concentration of one of the reactants – also known as volumetric analysis

trigonal pyramidal: the shape a molecule with four atoms can take up, e.g. NH_3

valency: indicates the number of bonds an atom of an element can form with atoms of another element

volatility: how easy it is for a liquid to form a gas – the more volatile a liquid is, the easier it is for it to form a gas

National 5
CHEMISTRY
For SQA 2019 and beyond

Leckie
the education publisher for Scotland

Practice Papers

Bob Wilson and Maria D'Arcy

Introduction

The two papers included in this section are designed to provide practice in the National 5 Chemistry course assessment question paper (the examination), which is worth 80% of the final grade for this course.

Together, the two papers give overall and comprehensive coverage of the assessment of **knowledge and its application** as well as the **skills of scientific inquiry** needed to pass National 5 Chemistry.

We recommend that candidates download a copy of the National 5 course specification from the SQA website. Print pages (18–20) which summarise the knowledge and skills which will be tested.

Design of the papers

Each paper has been carefully assembled to be very similar to a typical National 5 question paper. Each paper has 100 marks and is divided into two sections.

- **Section 1** – objective test, which contains 25 multiple choice items worth 1 mark each, totalling 25 marks.

- **Section 2** – paper 2, which contains restricted and extended response questions worth 1 to 3 marks each, totalling 75 marks.

In each paper, the marks are distributed evenly across all three areas of chemistry studied in the course, and the majority of the marks are for the demonstration and application of knowledge. The other marks are for the application of skills of scientific inquiry. We have included open and closed reading questions and have built in opportunities for candidates to suggest adjustments to experimental designs.

Most questions in each paper are set at the standard of Grade C, but there are also more difficult questions set at the standard for Grade A. We have attempted to construct each paper to represent the typical range of demand in a National 5 Chemistry paper.

Using the papers

We recommend working between attempting the questions and studying their expected answers online at www.leckieandleckie.co.uk.

You will need a **pen**, a **sharp pencil**, a **clear plastic ruler** and a **calculator** for the best results. A couple of different **coloured highlighters** could also be handy.

Expected answers

The expected answers online at www.leckieandleckie.co.uk give national standard answers but, occasionally, there may be other acceptable answers. The answers have Top Tips provided alongside each one but don't feel you need to use them all!

The Top Tips include hints on the chemistry itself as well as some memory ideas, a focus on traditionally difficult areas, advice on the wording of answers and notes of commonly made errors.

Grading

The two papers are designed to be equally demanding and to reflect the national standard of a typical SQA paper. Each paper has 100 marks – if you score 50 marks, that's a C pass. You will need about 60 marks for a B pass and about 70 marks for an A. **These figures are a rough guide only.**

Timing

If you are attempting a full paper, limit yourself to **two hours and 30 minutes** to complete. Get someone to time you! We recommend no more than 40 minutes for **Section 1** and the remainder of the time for **Section 2**.

If you are tackling blocks of questions, give yourself about a minute and a half per mark, for example, 10 marks of questions should take no longer than 15 minutes.

Good luck!

Practice paper A

N5 Chemistry

Practice Papers for SQA Exams
Paper A

Fill in these boxes:

Full name of centre

Town

Forename(s)

Surname

Try to answer all of the questions in the time allowed.

Total marks – 100

Section 1 – 25 marks

Section 2 – 75 marks

Read all questions carefully before attempting.

You have 2 hours and 30 minutes to complete this paper.

Write your answers in the spaces provided, including all of your working.

✕Leckie
the education publisher
for Scotland

SECTION 1

1. A gas is given off when zinc reacts with hydrochloric acid.

    An increase in which of the following would result in a slower reaction?

    A   temperature

    B   particle size

    C   concentration of the acid

    D   mass of the zinc

2. Which line in the table correctly describes an electron?

	Mass (atomic mass units)	Charge
A	almost zero	$+1$
B	almost zero	-1
C	1	$+1$
D	1	zero

3. Which of the following compounds contains ionic bonds?

    A   Nitrogen hydride

    B   Aluminium chloride

    C   Carbon tetrachloride

    D   Sulfur dioxide

4. Which of the following elements usually exist as diatomic molecules?

    A   Carbon

    B   Fluorine

    C   Krypton

    D   Phosphorus

5. A pupil set up the following apparatus.

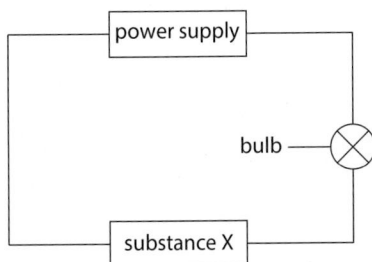

Which of the following substances would allow the bulb to light?

You may wish to use your data booklet to help you.

A NaCl(s)

B C_8H_{18}(l)

C Hg(l)

D SiO_2(s)

6. Which electron arrangement is that of an element which is very stable?

A 2,1

B 2,8,7

C 2,8,8

D 2,2

7. A molecule of silane is shown below.

The shape of a molecule of silane is

A linear

B angular

C tetrahedral

D trigonal pyramidal.

8. To neutralise 20 cm³ of a 1 mol l⁻¹ solution of sodium hydroxide requires 40 cm³ of HCl. What is the concentration of the HCl(aq)?

$$NaOH(aq) + HCl(aq) \longrightarrow NaCl(aq) + H_2O(l)$$

A $0 \cdot 1 \text{ mol l}^{-1}$

B $0 \cdot 2 \text{ mol l}^{-1}$

C $0 \cdot 05 \text{ mol l}^{-1}$

D $0 \cdot 5 \text{ mol l}^{-1}$

9. Chlorine has a number of isotopes. Each isotope **must** have

A   the same atomic number

B   the same mass number

C   different electron arrangements

D   different atomic and mass numbers.

10. What is the name of the following alkane?

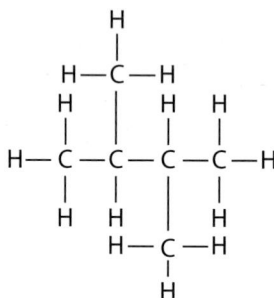

A   2,3-methylbutane

B   2,3-dimethylbutane

C   2,2-dimethylbutane

D   2,3-dimethylhexane

11. Which of the following could be the molecular formula for a cycloalkane?

A C_5H_6

B C_5H_8

C C_5H_{10}

D C_5H_{12}

12. Which of the following reactions can be described as combustion?

A $\quad 2H_2 + O_2 \longrightarrow 2H_2O$

B $\quad C_2H_4 + H_2 \longrightarrow C_2H_6$

C $\quad C_3H_6 + H_2O \longrightarrow C_3H_7OH$

D $\quad C_8H_{18} \longrightarrow C_3H_6 + C_5H_{12}$

13. Alkenes react with bromine.

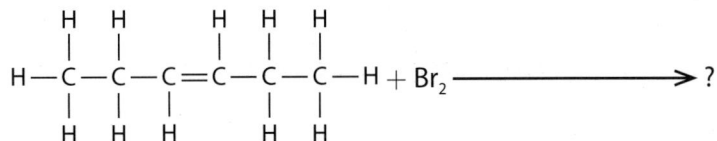

$$
\begin{array}{c}
\quad\; H \;\; H \qquad\; H \;\; H \;\; H \\
\quad\; | \;\;\; | \qquad\; | \;\;\; | \;\;\; | \\
H-C-C-C=C-C-C-H + Br_2 \longrightarrow ? \\
\quad\; | \;\;\; | \;\;\; | \qquad | \;\;\; | \\
\quad\; H \;\; H \;\; H \qquad H \;\; H
\end{array}
$$

Identify the product of the above reaction.

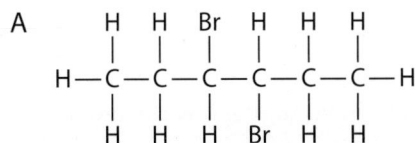

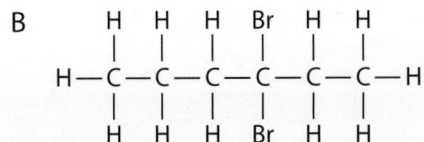

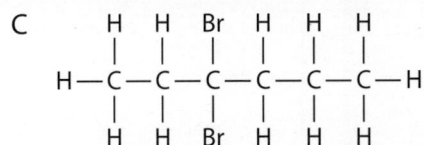

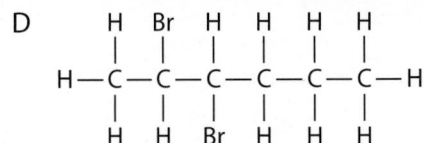

A
$$
\begin{array}{c}
\;\; H \;\; H \;\; Br \;\; H \;\; H \;\; H \\
\;\; | \;\;\; | \;\;\; | \;\;\; | \;\;\; | \;\;\; | \\
H-C-C-C-C-C-C-H \\
\;\; | \;\;\; | \;\;\; | \;\;\; | \;\;\; | \;\;\; | \\
\;\; H \;\; H \;\; H \;\; Br \;\; H \;\; H
\end{array}
$$

B
$$
\begin{array}{c}
\;\; H \;\; H \;\; H \;\; Br \;\; H \;\; H \\
\;\; | \;\;\; | \;\;\; | \;\;\; | \;\;\; | \;\;\; | \\
H-C-C-C-C-C-C-H \\
\;\; | \;\;\; | \;\;\; | \;\;\; | \;\;\; | \;\;\; | \\
\;\; H \;\; H \;\; H \;\; Br \;\; H \;\; H
\end{array}
$$

C
$$
\begin{array}{c}
\;\; H \;\; H \;\; Br \;\; H \;\; H \;\; H \\
\;\; | \;\;\; | \;\;\; | \;\;\; | \;\;\; | \;\;\; | \\
H-C-C-C-C-C-C-H \\
\;\; | \;\;\; | \;\;\; | \;\;\; | \;\;\; | \;\;\; | \\
\;\; H \;\; H \;\; Br \;\; H \;\; H \;\; H
\end{array}
$$

D
$$
\begin{array}{c}
\;\; H \;\; Br \;\; H \;\; H \;\; H \;\; H \\
\;\; | \;\;\; | \;\;\; | \;\;\; | \;\;\; | \;\;\; | \\
H-C-C-C-C-C-C-H \\
\;\; | \;\;\; | \;\;\; | \;\;\; | \;\;\; | \;\;\; | \\
\;\; H \;\; H \;\; Br \;\; H \;\; H \;\; H
\end{array}
$$

14. Which of the following is a use of carboxylic acids?

A   fuel

B   fertiliser

C   solvents

D   preservatives

15. Which line in the table below matches the family of compounds to its correct functional group?

	Family	Functional group
A	Alcohol	OH
B	Alkene	COOH
C	Carboxylic acid	OH
D	Cycloalkane	COOH

16. Which of the following substances reacts with hydrochloric acid to make a gas that turns limewater cloudy?

A Magnesium carbonate

B Magnesium

C Silver oxide

D Silver

17. Which of the following metals would result in an increase in voltage if it was used in place of copper in the following cell?

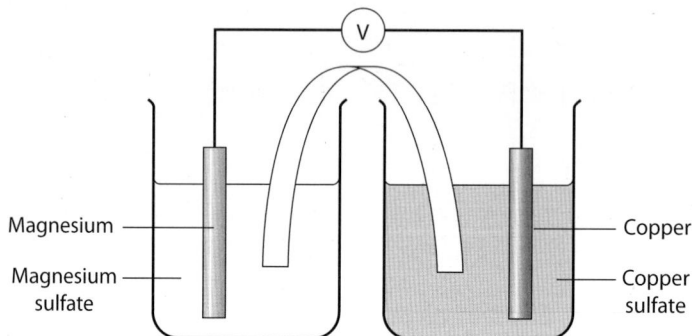

A Aluminium

B Gold

C Iron

D Lead

18. Which of the following metals can only be extracted from its ore by electrolysis?

A Copper

B Lead

C Silver

D Sodium

19. Iron can be extracted from its ore in a blast furnace.

$$Fe_2O_3(s) + CO(g) \longrightarrow Fe(s) + CO_2(g)$$

Which species is the reducing agent?

A $Fe_2O_3(s)$

B $CO(g)$

C $Fe(s)$

D $CO_2(g)$

20. Which of the following metals would react with zinc bromide?

A   Copper

B   Lead

C   Magnesium

D   Tin

21. Four cells were made by joining silver to copper, iron, magnesium and tin.

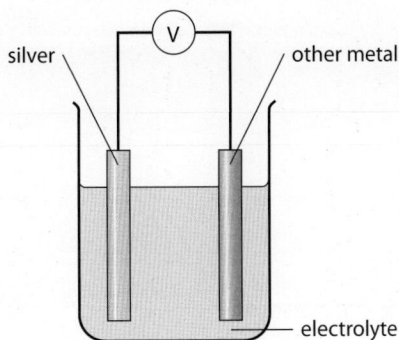

The voltages for the four cells are shown in the table.

Which cell contained silver joined to magnesium?

You may wish to use your data booklet to help you.

Cell	Voltage (V)
A	1·8
B	1·3
C	0·9
D	0·6

22. The structure below shows a section of a polymer.

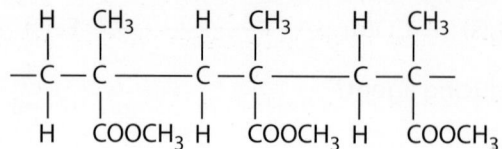

$$\begin{array}{cccccc} H & CH_3 & H & CH_3 & H & CH_3 \\ | & | & | & | & | & | \\ -C-C- & \!\!\!\!\!\!\!\!\!\! & C-C- & \!\!\!\!\!\!\!\!\!\! & C-C- \\ | & | & | & | & | & | \\ H & COOCH_3 & H & COOCH_3 & H & COOCH_3 \end{array}$$

Which of the following structures represents the repeating unit in the polymer.

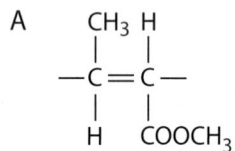

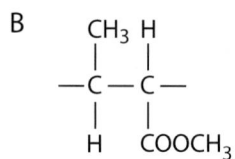

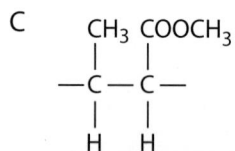

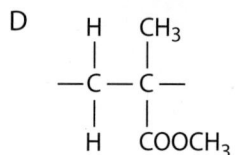

A
$$\begin{array}{cc} CH_3 & H \\ | & | \\ -C=C- \\ | & | \\ H & COOCH_3 \end{array}$$

B
$$\begin{array}{cc} CH_3 & H \\ | & | \\ -C-C- \\ | & | \\ H & COOCH_3 \end{array}$$

C
$$\begin{array}{cc} CH_3 & COOCH_3 \\ | & | \\ -C-C- \\ | & | \\ H & H \end{array}$$

D
$$\begin{array}{cc} H & CH_3 \\ | & | \\ -C-C- \\ | & | \\ H & COOCH_3 \end{array}$$

23. The catalyst used in the Haber process is

A   Platinum

B   Iron

C   Copper

D   Gold.

24. Different types of radiation have different penetrating properties.

Which type of radiation(s) can be stopped by a thin sheet of aluminium?

A   Alpha only

B   Beta only

C   Alpha and Beta

D   Alpha, Beta and Gamma

25. An unknown solid substance, substance x, was analysed.

1.   It neutralises hydrochloric acid, producing a gas.

2.   It burns to give off a blue-green colour.

Substance X could be:

You may wish to use your data booklet to help you.

A   Copper

B   Barium oxide

C   Copper carbonate

D   Nickel hydroxide

N5 Chemistry

Practice Papers for SQA Exams

Paper A

Fill in these boxes:

Full name of centre

Town

Forename(s)

Surname

Section 2 – 75 marks

Attempt all questions.

×Leckie
the education publisher
for Scotland

SECTION 2

1. When magnesium reacts with hydrochloric acid, hydrogen gas is given off.

   The rate of the reaction can be followed by measuring the volume of hydrogen, $H_2(g)$, evolved.

   The table shows the volume of gas given off when excess hydrochloric acid, HCl, is reacted with 0·08 g of magnesium.

Time (s)	Volume of gas (cm³)
0	0
10	14
20	38
40	59
60	69
80	70
100	70

   (a) Plot a line graph of the results of the reaction.   3

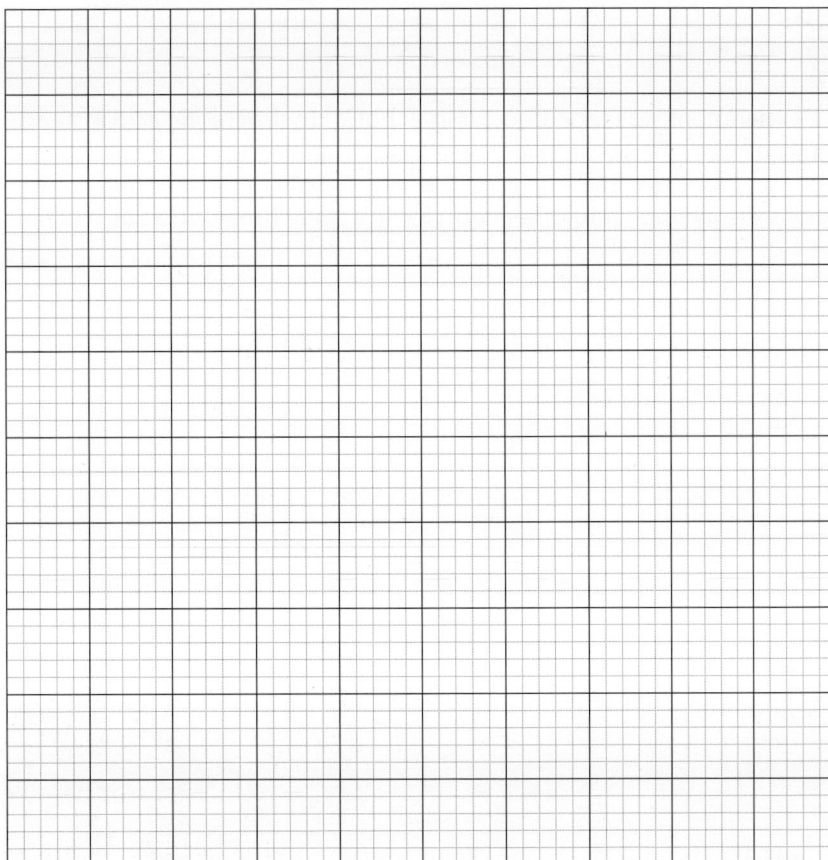

(b) The average rate of the reaction can be measured using data from the graph.

(i) Calculate the rate of the reaction between 10 seconds and 40 seconds. **3**

Your answer must include the appropriate unit.

Show your working clearly.

(ii) The experiment was repeated using 2 mol l^{-1} hydrochloric acid instead of 1 mol l^{-1}.

Predict the average rate of reaction for the same time period as b (i). **1**

2. Copper is found in the ore Chalcopyrite, $CuFeS_2$.

The iron is removed from the ore to form copper(I)sulfide.

(a) Write the ionic formula for copper(I)sulfide.

1

(b) When a sample of copper was analysed it was found to be a mixture of two isotopes, ^{63}Cu and ^{65}Cu. The relative atomic mass of copper is 63·5.

Which isotope is the most common?

1

(c) Copper can form charged particles such as

$$^{63}_{29}Cu^{2+}$$

(i) What name is given to a charged particle like the one above?

1

(ii) Calculate the number of protons, neutrons and electrons which are in the above charged particle.

2

Subatomic particle	Number
Protons	
Neutrons	
Electrons	

3. A pupil analysed a sample of carbon (graphite) and found it to have a high melting point and to conduct electricity as a solid.

The pupil concluded that graphite must have metallic bonding.

Using your knowledge of chemistry, discuss the pupil's conclusion.

3

4. Read the passage below and answer the questions which follow.

Ocean acidification

When carbon dioxide (CO_2) is absorbed by sea water, chemical reactions occur that reduce sea water pH, carbonate ion concentration and saturation states of biologically important calcium carbonate minerals. These chemical reactions are termed 'ocean acidification' or 'OA' for short.

Carbon dioxide dissolves in sea water to form carbonic acid (H_2CO_3), which releases some of its hydrogen ions into the sea water. Some of these hydrogen ions then bind to carbonate (CO_3^{2-}) ions in the sea to form bicarbonate ions (HCO_3^-), decreasing the amount of carbonate ions in the water. Since industrialisation (in the 1800s), surface ocean carbonate ion concentrations have declined by 10 per cent in the tropics and southern oceans.

Ocean acidification is expected to impact ocean species to varying degrees. Photosynthetic algae and sea grasses may benefit from higher CO_2 conditions in the ocean as they require CO_2 to live, just like plants on land. On the other hand, studies have shown that a more acidic environment has a dramatic effect on some calcifying species such as oysters, corals and molluscs.

Calcium carbonate minerals are the building blocks for the skeletons and shells of many marine organisms. In areas where most life now congregates in the ocean, the sea water is supersaturated with respect to calcium carbonate minerals. This means there are abundant building blocks for calcifying organisms to build their skeletons and shells. However, continued ocean acidification is causing many parts of the ocean to become undersaturated with these minerals, which is likely to affect the ability of some organisms to produce and maintain their shells.

This passage was based on an article by the 'Yale Climate Media Forum', http://www.yaleclimatemediaforum. org/2008/06/covering-ocean-acidification-chemistry-and-considerations.

(a) CO_2(g) forms carbonic acid H_2CO_3(aq) when absorbed by sea water.
What evidence is there to show how this acid lowers the pH of the sea? **1**

(b) Give **one** way in which ocean acidification has benefited some ocean species. **1**

(c) Since the 1800s the level of industrialisation has grown and therefore the use of alkane based fuels has increased. Explain why this has resulted in an decrease in pH levels in the ocean. **1**

5. The concentration of hydrochloric acid is often determined by reacting it with a known concentration of sodium carbonate.

The equation for the reaction is:

$$Na^+_2CO^{2-}_3(aq) + 2H^+Cl^-(aq) \longrightarrow CO_2(g) + 2Na^+Cl^-(aq) + H_2O(l)$$

(a) Circle the spectator ions in the above equation.

1

(b) An accurate solution used to determine the concentration of another is often called a standard solution.

   (i) Calculate the number of moles of sodium carbonate required to make 250 cm^3 of a 0·1 mol l^{-1} solution.

      Show your working clearly.

2

   (ii) Using your answer to part (i), calculate the mass of sodium carbonate (Na_2CO_3) needed to make 250 cm^3 of a 0·1 mol l^{-1} solution of sodium carbonate.

      Show your working clearly.

2

(c) Two students prepared the standard solution of sodium carbonate using a 250 cm^3 volumetric flask.

The notes on the next page were taken from their lab books.

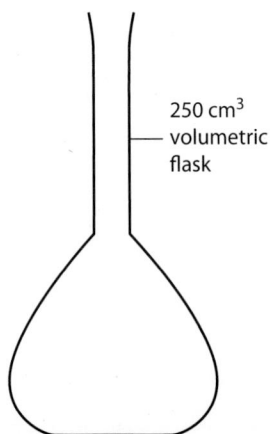

250 cm^3
volumetric
flask

Student A	Student B
The correct mass of sodium carbonate was weighed out in a beaker.	The correct mass of sodium hydrogen carbonate was weighed out in a beaker.
50 cm^3 of water was added and then stirred with a stirring rod until all the sodium carbonate had dissolved.	50 cm^3 of water was added and then stirred with a stirring rod until all the sodium carbonate had dissolved.
The solution was then transferred to a 250 cm^3 standard flask.	The solution was then transferred to a 250 cm^3 flask.
A further 50 cm^3 of water was added to the beaker, stirred and then added to the standard flask.	A further 50 cm^3 of water was added to the beaker, stirred and then added to the standard flask.
Water was then added up to the 250 cm^3 mark on the standard flask.	150 cm^3 of water was then added to the flask.

Explain which student would have prepared a more accurate solution of sodium carbonate.

2

6. A pupil carried out an experiment to measure the energy released when pentane (C_5H_{12}) is burned.

The pupil set up the apparatus below.

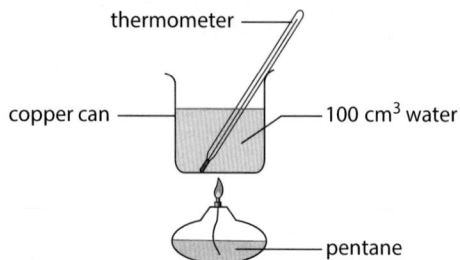

The student recorded the following data:

Mass of pentane	2 g
Volume of water	100 cm^3
Initial temperature of water	21 $^\circ$C
Final temperature of water	29 $^\circ$C
Specific heat capacity of water	4·18 kJkg$^{-1\circ}$C^{-1}

(a) Calculate the energy released, in kJ.

   Show your working clearly.

3

(b) Suggest an improvement that could be made to make the experiment more accurate.

1

(c) Pentane belongs to the alkanes.

(i) What is the general formula of the alkanes?

1

(ii) Draw an isomer of the pentane molecule shown below.

1

$$H-\overset{\overset{\displaystyle H}{|}}{\underset{\underset{\displaystyle H}{|}}{C}}-\overset{\overset{\displaystyle H}{|}}{\underset{\underset{\displaystyle H}{|}}{C}}-\overset{\overset{\displaystyle H}{|}}{\underset{\underset{\displaystyle H}{|}}{C}}-\overset{\overset{\displaystyle H}{|}}{\underset{\underset{\displaystyle H}{|}}{C}}-\overset{\overset{\displaystyle H}{|}}{\underset{\underset{\displaystyle H}{|}}{C}}-H$$

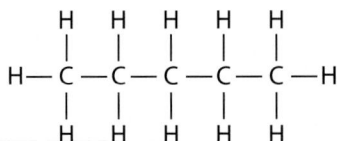

(d) The chemical products from the combustion of pentane are water and gas X. The water can be collected in a test tube placed in an ice water bath.

(i) Complete the diagram to show the apparatus needed to collect the water vapour and allow the gas X to be bubbled through the limewater.

2

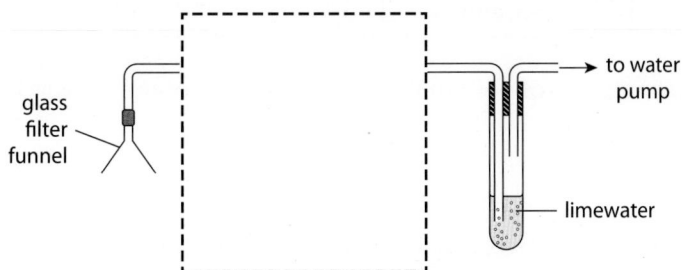

(ii) Gas X turns the limewater cloudy.

Identify gas X.

1

7. The aldehydes are carbon compounds that contain the carbonyl, $C=O$ group at the end of the chain of carbon atoms.

The full structural formula for the first three members is shown below.

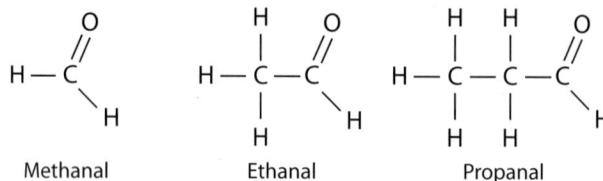

Methanal   Ethanal   Propanal

(a) (i) Draw the full structural formula for butanal. **1**

(ii) The aldehydes are an example of a homologous series.
What is meant by the term homologous series? **1**

(b) The boiling points of some aldehydes are listed below.

Aldehydes	Boiling point (°C)
ethanal	20
propanal	49
butanal	76
pentanal	

Predict the boiling point of pentanal, the fifth member of the aldehyde family. **1**

(c) Aldehydes can be made by oxidising alcohols. The reaction is shown below.

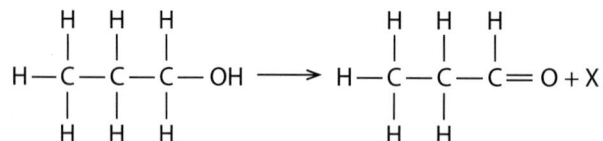

(i) What is element X? **1**

(ii) Explain why propan-2-ol cannot be oxidised into an aldehyde. **1**

8. (a) Carboxylic acids react with alkalis to produce salt and water.

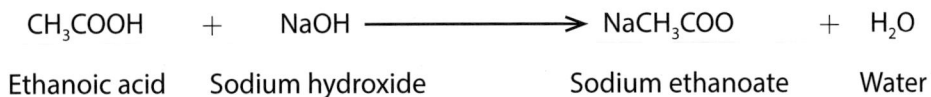

CH_3COOH + $NaOH$ ⟶ $NaCH_3COO$ + H_2O

Ethanoic acid   Sodium hydroxide   Sodium ethanoate   Water

(i) What mass of water would be produced if 1·5 g of ethanoic acid was reacted completely with sodium hydroxide?

Show your working clearly.

3

(ii) Name the salt that would be produced when ethanoic acid reacts with potassium hydroxide.

1

(b) Sodium ethanoate and ethanoic acid are mixed to make the flavouring that goes into salt and vinegar crisps.

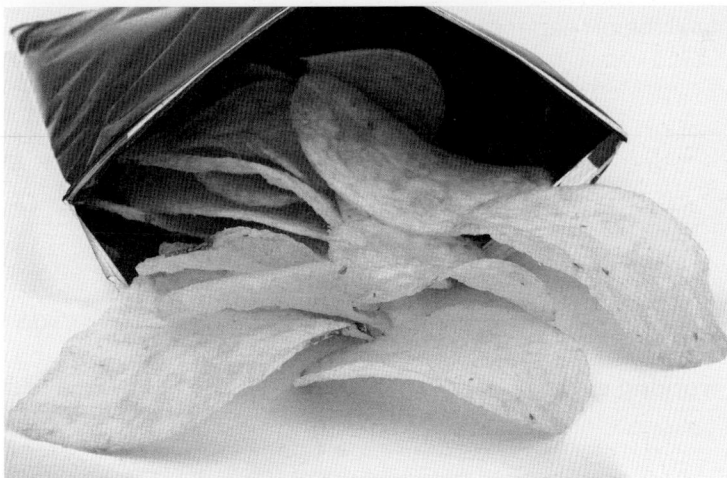

Give another use for ethanoic acid.

1

9. Ammonia can be produced in the laboratory.

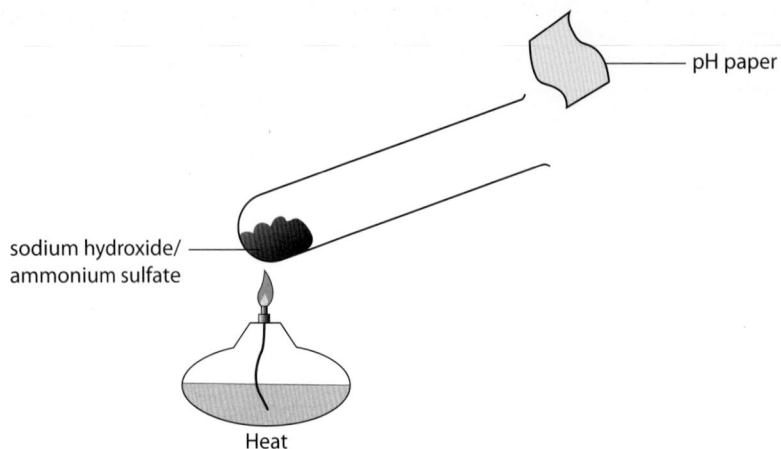

The reaction occurring in the above apparatus is:

$$(NH_4)_2SO_4\ (s) + NaOH(s) \longrightarrow Na_2SO_4(s) + NH_3(g) + H_2O(l)$$

(a) Balance the equation. **1**

(b) What colour will the pH paper turn? **1**

(c) Calculate the percentage by mass of nitrogen in ammonium sulfate $(NH_4)_2SO_4$. **3**

   Show your working clearly.

(d) (i) Ammonia is one of the starting materials in the industrial manufacture of nitric acid. A mixture of ammonia and air is passed over a catalyst at between 600–900°C. The reaction is very exothermic.

Suggest why the reaction being exothermic is an advantage in this process. **2**

(ii) State why catalysts are used in chemical reactions. **1**

(e) One of the major uses of ammonia and nitric acid is in the manufacture of ammonium nitrate (NH_4NO_3).

State why ammonium nitrate is widely used as a fertiliser. **1**

10. The Voyager 2 satellite has been sending scientific information about our solar system back to Earth for the last 36 years.

Plutonium 238 fuels the satellite.

(a) Plutonium 238 has a half life of 87·7 years.

   (i)   State what is meant by the term half life.

   1

   (ii)   How long would it take for a 20 g sample of Plutonium 238 to decay to 1·25 g?   **2**

   (iii)   Voyager 2 has had to function under extreme temperatures.

   State what effect this will have had on the half life of plutonium 238.

   1

(b) The nuclear equation for the decay of Plutonium 238 is shown below.

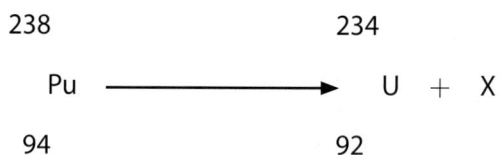

$$^{238}_{94}Pu \longrightarrow {}^{234}_{92}U + X$$

   (i)   Name particle X.

   1

   (ii)   Give **one** reason why Plutonium 238 is a suitable radioactive isotope to fuel the satellite.

   1

MARKS
Do not write in this margin

11. Oils and fats are found in many foods. Both oils and fats contain fatty acids. The types of fatty acid found in fats and oils are shown below.

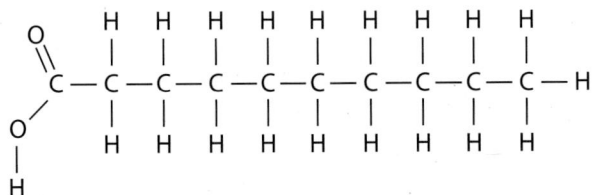

Fat

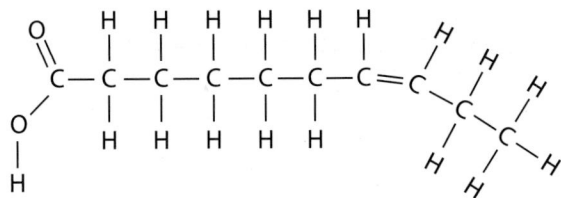

Oil

Using your knowledge of chemistry, discuss the differences and/or similarities in the chemical properties of the fatty acids in an oil and fat.

3

12. Car manufacturers have developed cars that are powered by hydrogen fuel cells.

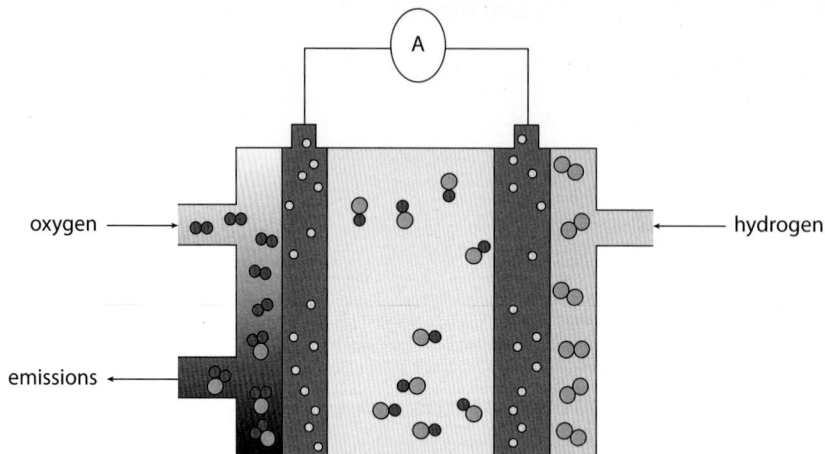

(a) The reaction that takes place at the hydrogen electrode is shown below.

$$H_2(g) \longrightarrow 2H^+(aq) + 2e$$

(i) What name is given to this type of reaction?

1

(ii) The following reaction takes place at the oxygen electrode.

$$O_2(g) + 4H^+(aq) + 4e \longrightarrow 2H_2O(l)$$

Write the balanced redox equation for the hydrogen fuel cell.

1

(iii) On the diagram, clearly mark the path and direction of electron flow.

1

13. Polymethylmethacrylate (Perspex) is often used as a substitute for glass and is used to make dentures.

The monomer methylmethacrylate is shown below.

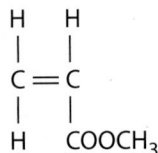

$$\begin{array}{c}
\quad H \quad\; H \\
\quad | \quad\;\; | \\
\quad C = C \\
\quad | \quad\;\; | \\
\quad H \quad COOCH_3
\end{array}$$

(a) Draw a section of the polymer polymethylmethacrylate, showing three monomers joined together.

1

(b) What type of polymerisation takes place to make Perspex?

1

(c) The first contact lenses were hard and made from polymethylmethacrylate. Hydroxyl groups were added to the polymer, making it softer and capable of absorbing water.

This development led to soft contact lenses, which we use today.

(i) Circle the hydroxyl group in the monomer hydroxylethylmethacrylate.

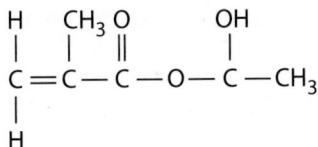

1

$$\begin{array}{c}
\quad H \quad\; CH_3\; O \qquad\;\; OH \\
\quad | \quad\;\; | \quad\;\; || \qquad\;\;\; | \\
\quad C = C - C - O - C - CH_3 \\
\quad | \\
\quad H
\end{array}$$

(ii) Apart from the hydroxyl group, name one other functional group present in the above molecules of hydroxylethylmethacrylate?

1

14. The work card below details how the volume of acid needed to neutralise an alkali can be found. Steps 2 and 6 are missing.

Neutralisation Work Card

Method

1. Add exactly 25 cm^3 of the alkali to a conical flask.

2.

3. Add acid to the burette and note the reading.

4. Add acid to the alkali while swirling the conical flask.

5. Stop adding the acid when the end-point is reached.

6.

(a) Complete the work card by giving instructions for steps 2 and 6.   **2**

Step 2:

Step 6:

(b) Name the piece of glassware used to transfer the alkali to the conical flask in step 1.   **1**

(c) What name is given to the analytical technique detailed in the work card.   **1**

(d) When a base is neutralised by an acid water and a salt is formed.

    (i)   Name the salt produced when potassium hydroxide is neutralised by sulfuric acid.   **1**

    (ii)   State how you could obtain a solid sample of the salt produced.   **1**

Practice paper B

N5 Chemistry

Practice Papers for SQA Exams   Paper B

Fill in these boxes:

Full name of centre   Town

Forename(s)   Surname

Try to answer all of the questions in the time allowed.

Total marks – 100

Section 1 – 25 marks

Section 2 – 75 marks

Read all questions carefully before attempting.

You have 2 hours and 30 minutes to complete this paper.

Write your answers in the spaces provided, including all of your working.

×Leckie
the education publisher
for Scotland

SECTION 1

1. In some countries fluorine is used to reduce tooth decay. Fluorine is an example of

    A   a noble gas

    B   an alkali metal

    C   a halogen

    D   a transition element.

2. What is the symbol for the element which has an ion with the same electron arrangement as neon?

    A   Li

    B   Cl

    C   N

    D   K

3. The table gives information about some particles.

    Identify the particle which is an ion with a 2^+ charge.

Particle	protons	neutrons	electrons
A	9	10	10
B	11	12	10
C	15	16	15
D	20	20	18

4. Atoms in the same group in the periodic table have the same

    A   atomic number

    B   number of outer electrons

    C   number of protons

    D   number of neutrons

5. Which of the following compounds is made up of three elements?

    A   Silicon dioxide

    B   Magnesium nitride

    C   Ammonium hydride

    D   Sodium sulfate

6. Which of the following types of compounds does not conduct electricity as a solid but does as a melt or in solution?

    A   covalent network

    B   ionic

    C   covalent discrete

    D   metallic

7. The shape of an ammonia molecule is shown below.

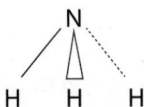

    What name is given to this shape?

    A   tetrahedral

    B   linear

    C   trigonal pyramidal

    D   angular

8. The bonds which make up a molecule of carbon dioxide (CO_2) can be represented as:

    $$O = C = O$$

    A molecule of carbon dioxide consists of:

    A   two single covalent bonds

    B   a single and a triple bond

    C   four single covalent bonds

    D   two double covalent bonds.

9. What is the name of the compound with the formula Ag_2S?

 A Silver(I) sulfide

 B Silver(II) sulfide

 C Silver(III) sulfide

 D Silver(IV) sulfide

10. Which of the following substances forms an alkali when added to water?
You may wish to use your data booklet to help you.

 A Aluminium oxide

 B Sulfur dioxide

 C Sodium oxide

 D Carbon dioxide

11. Copper hydroxide can be prepared by reacting copper nitrate and sodium hydroxide.

$$Cu(NO_3)_2(aq) + NaOH(aq) \longrightarrow Cu(OH)_2(s) + NaNO_3(aq)$$

Copper hydroxide can be separated from the reaction mixture by

 A evaporating the solution

 B filtering the solution

 C boiling the mixture

 D distilling the mixture.

12. Which of the following statements correctly describes the concentrations of $H^+(aq)$ and $OH^-(aq)$ ions in an acid?

 A The concentrations of $H^+(aq)$ and $OH^-(aq)$ ions are equal.

 B The concentrations of $H^+(aq)$ and $OH^-(aq)$ ions are zero.

 C The concentration of $H^+(aq)$ ions is greater than the concentration of $OH^-(aq)$ ions.

 D The concentration of $H^+(aq)$ ions is lower than the concentration of $OH^-(aq)$ ions.

13. Which line in the table describes what happens when water is added to an alkali?

	pH	OH⁻ ion concentration
A	increases	increases
B	decreases	decreases
C	increases	decreases
D	decreases	increases

14. Which of the following hydrocarbons has the highest boiling point?

You may wish to use your data booklet to help you.

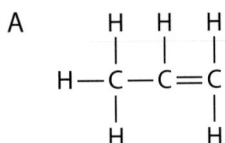

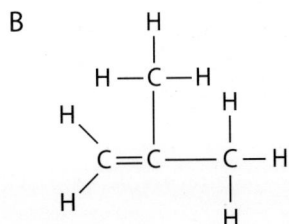

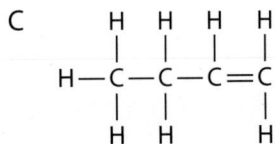

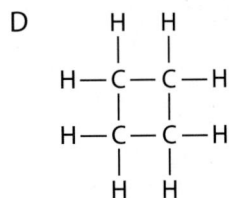

A

```
        H   H   H
        |   |   |
    H—C—C═C
        |       |
        H       H
```

B

```
            H
            |
        H—C—H
            |       H
    H\      |       |
      C═C——C—H
    H/      |       |
            H
```

C

```
        H   H   H   H
        |   |   |   |
    H—C—C—C═C
        |   |       |
        H   H       H
```

D

```
        H   H
        |   |
    H—C—C—H
        |   |
    H—C—C—H
        |   |
        H   H
```

15. Which of the following hydrocarbons is an isomer of 2-methylhexane?

A

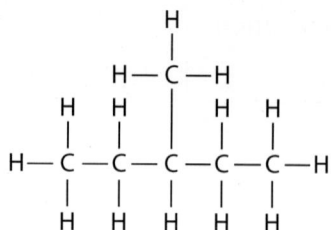

B

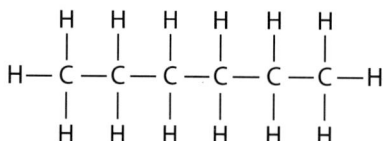

C

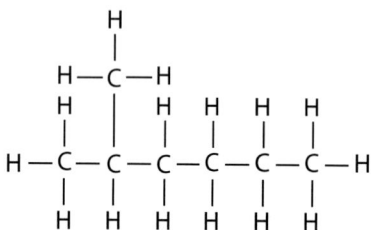

D

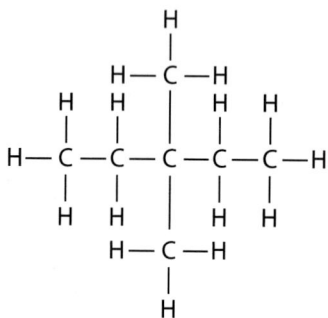

16. The name given to the family of compounds with the general formula C_nH_{2n} is

A   Alkanes

B   Alcohols

C   Cycloalkanes

D   Carboxylic acids.

17. What is the name of the compound below?

$$CH_3CH_2COOH$$

    A   Ethanol

    B   Ethanoic acid

    C   Propanol

    D   Propanoic acid

18. Which of the following hydrocarbons could be described as saturated?

    A C_2H_2

    B C_2H_4

    C C_2H_6

    D C_3H_4

19. Which of the following metals can be found uncombined in nature?

    A   Aluminium

    B   Copper

    C   Gold

    D   Tin

20. Metal X can be obtained from its oxide by heating with carbon but not by heating alone. Metal X does not react with acids but will react with silver nitrate. Metal X could be:

    A   Iron

    B   Copper

    C   Magnesium

    D   Platinum.

21. Iron can be extracted from its oxide by reacting it with carbon monoxide.

$$Fe_2O_3(s) + 3CO(g) \longrightarrow 2Fe(s) + 3CO_2(g)$$

The reducing agent in the above reaction is

A $CO_2(g)$

B $Fe_2O_3(s)$

C $CO(g)$

D $Fe(s)$.

22. Which of the following would be a suitable fertiliser?

You may wish to use your data booklet

A   Barium phosphate

B   Nickel phosphate

C   Ammonium sulphate

D   Barium sulphate

23. A radioisotope is used to measure the thickness of paper. Paper is passed under a radioactive source. If the paper is too thick, the intensity of the radiation decreases and the paper is stopped.

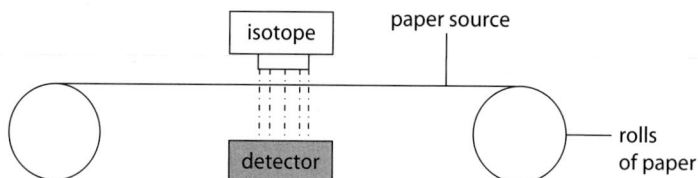

Which isotope would make a suitable source?

Radio isotopes	Half life	Source
A	Long	Alpha
B	Long	Beta
C	Short	Alpha
D	Short	Beta

24. The catalyst used in the production of ammonia is

    A   Platinum

    B   Aluminium oxide

    C   Iron

    D   Titanium.

25. Oxygen gas

    A   burns with a pop

    B   relights a glowing splint

    C   turns damp pH paper blue

    D   turns limewater cloudy.

N5 Chemistry

Practice Papers for SQA Exams   Paper B

Fill in these boxes:

Full name of centre   Town

Forename(s)   Surname

Section 2 – 75 marks

Attempt all questions.

Leckie
the education publisher
for Scotland

SECTION 2

1. Aluminium carbonate is one of a number of chemicals used to treat conditions caused by excessive stomach acid, such as heartburn and ulcers. The main acid in stomach acid is hydrochloric acid.

The reaction between aluminium carbonate and hydrochloric acid is shown below.

$$Al_2(CO_3)_3(s) + HCl(aq) \longrightarrow AlCl_3(aq) + H_2O(l) + CO_2(g)$$

(a) Balance the above equation.

1

The speed of the reaction can be followed by measuring the loss in mass.

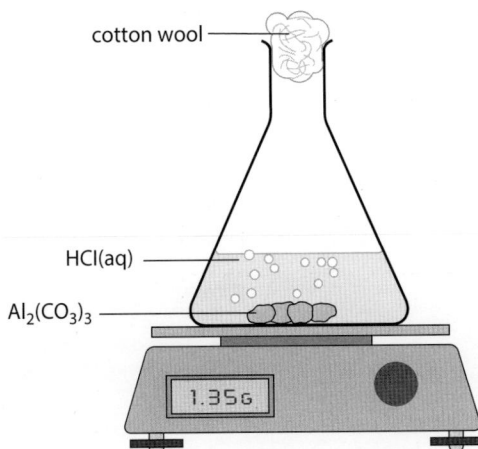

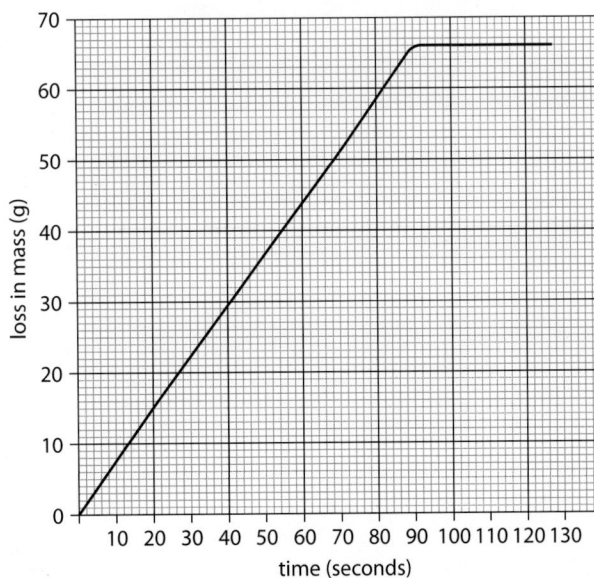

cotton wool

HCl(aq)

$Al_2(CO_3)_3$

1.35 g

(b) (i) During the reaction the mass of the reacting mixture decreases.

Explain why the loss in mass occurs?

1

(ii) Using the graph, calculate the average rate of reaction between 20 seconds and 70 seconds.

3

Your answer must include the appropriate unit.

Show your working clearly.

(iii) The rate of reaction decreases with time.

Explain why the rate of the reaction decreases as the reaction proceeds.

1

2. (a) Francium, the last natural element, was discovered in 1939.

An ion of this element was found to contain:

87 protons

136 neutrons

86 electrons.

   (i) Using the information above, determine the atomic number and mass number.

   Atomic number _____

   Mass number _____   **1**

   (ii) Represent this information in the form of a nuclide notation, by filling in the boxes below.   **1**

$$\boxed{\begin{array}{c} \\ \hline \end{array}} \ Fr^+$$

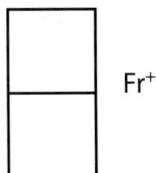

   (iii) What is the charge on this ion of Francium?   **1**

(b) Francium has 33 different isotopes.

   What is meant by the word isotope?   **1**

3. Graphene is a flat sheet of carbon atoms just one atom thick. It is 100 times stronger than steel, more conductive than copper and more flexible than rubber. One way of producing graphene is to heat silicon carbide to over 1100 °C.

(a) Describe a test you could carry out on graphene to show that it conducts electricity. **2**

(b) Suggest why graphene can conduct electricity. **1**

(c) Give the formula for silicon carbide. **1**

(d) Silicon and carbon are in the same group of the periodic table. They can form oxides with the similar formulae: carbon dioxide (CO_2) and silicon dioxide (SiO_2). Both silicon and carbon form covalent bonds with oxygen. Despite these similarities, their oxides have very different melting points and boiling points, as shown in the table.

Compound	Melting point (°C)	Boiling point (°C)
Carbon dioxide (CO_2)	−57	−78
Silicon dioxide (SiO_2)	1713	2950

Explain the difference in melting points and boiling points between the two compounds. **3**

4. Read the passage below and answer the following questions.

Oil spillage disasters a thing of the past

Scientists have manufactured a lightweight and reusable material that can absorb up to 33 times its weight in certain chemicals.

'Environmental protection is a globally important issue, especially with so many reports of oil spillage and contaminated rivers due to industry; says study co-author Professor Ian Chen from Deakin University.

Chen and colleagues have developed nanosheets of boron nitride, also called white graphene, which can soak up a wide range of spilled oils, chemical solvents and dyes, such as those discharged by the textile, paper and tannery industries.

Highly porous, the sheets have a high surface area, can float on water, and are water-repellent, the researchers report in the journal *Nature Communications*.

'This material has overall excellent performance compared to other materials;

'One gram of our material will absorb 30 grams of oil', says Chen.

Once the white sheets are dropped on an oil-polluted water surface they immediately absorb the brown oil and become dark brown.

'This process is very fast; after just two minutes, all the oil has been taken up by the nanosheets,' they write.

But rapid absorption isn't the only advantage, Chen says. Once saturated, the sheets can be easily picked up from the water surface and cleaned by burning, heating or washing, to be reused several times.

'Our material can be burned in air to clean all the absorbed oil.

You cannot do this with other carbon-based materials because you burn everything off.'

'After heating the oil-saturated material you can reuse the material again to reabsorb new oil'.

'The ability to recycle makes it a cost-effective alternative', he adds.

This passage was adapted from an article by 'ABC science', Wednesday, 1 May 2013.

(a) Suggest what type of bonding exists in the nanosheet made of boron nitride.

1

(b) How many grams of oil are absorbed by 10 grams of the nanosheet?

1

5. Tartaric acid is produced when red grapes grow and is the main acid in red wine. Too much tartaric acid will result in the wine being tart and of a poor quality. The concentration of tartaric acid in red wine can be determined by titrating with sodium hydroxide.

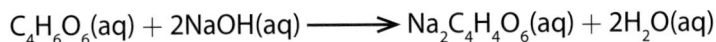

$$C_4H_6O_6(aq) + 2NaOH(aq) \longrightarrow Na_2C_4H_4O_6(aq) + 2H_2O(aq)$$

A pupil titrated 25 cm³ of red wine with 0·1 mol l⁻¹ sodium hydroxide. Her results are shown below.

	Titration 1	Titration 2	Titration 3
Volume of NaOH beginning (cm³)	0	12·8	21·7
Volume of NaOH end (cm³)	12·8	21·7	30·4
Total volume of NaOH added (cm³)	12·8	8·9	8·7

(a) Explain why the average volume of sodium hydroxide is taken as 8·8 and not 10·1 cm³.

1

(b) (i) Calculate the number of moles of tartaric acid in **25 cm³** of wine.

3

(ii) The concentration is recorded as g of tartaric acid per 25 cm³ of wine.

Calculate the mass of tartaric acid in g per 25 cm³ of wine.

2

6. Acids and alkalis can be classed as strong or weak.

Acid	pH	Classification
Nitric	1	Strong
Sulfuric	1	Strong
Carbonic	4	Weak
Ethanoic	4	Weak

Alkali	pH	Classification
Sodium hydroxide	14	Strong
Lithium hydroxide	14	Strong
Ammonium hydroxide	10	Weak

(a) Alkalis neutralise acids to form a variety of salts.

The name and pH of a number of salt solutions are shown below.

Name of salt	pH
Ammonium nitrate	4
Ammonium carbonate	7
Sodium sulfate	7
Sodium carbonate	9

(i) State the classification of acid and alkali that react together to form an acidic salt.

1

(ii) Predict the pH of the salt produced when lithium hydroxide reacts with sulfuric acid.

1

(b) A student investigated how the pH of an acid could be increased to 7, a neutral solution. Using your knowledge of chemistry, discuss how the pH of an acid could be increased to form a neutral solution by substances other than alkalis.

3

7. The alkynes are a group of compounds that contain a carbon to carbon triple bond.

H—C≡C—H	ethyne
H—C≡C—C—H (with H above and H below middle C)	propyne
H—C≡C—C—C—H (with H, H above and H, H below the two middle C)	but-1-yne
H—C—C≡C—C—H (with H above/H below first C and H above/H below last C)	but-2-yne
H—C≡C—C—C—C—H (with H, H, H above and H, H, H below the three middle C)	X

(a) (i) What is the general formula for the alkynes?

1

(ii) Suggest a name for X.

1

(b) The alkynes react with bromine as follows:

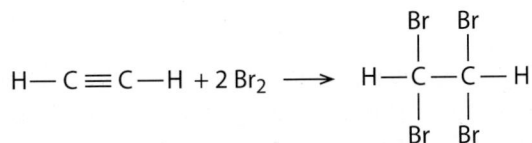

$$H—C≡C—H + 2\,Br_2 \longrightarrow \begin{array}{c} Br\ \ \ Br \\ |\ \ \ \ | \\ H—C—C—H \\ |\ \ \ \ | \\ Br\ \ \ Br \end{array}$$

(i) Draw the full structural formula of the product when but-1-yne fully reacts with bromine.

1

(ii) What name is given to this type of reaction?

1

8. (a) Industrial alcohols can be produced by passing alkenes and steam over a catalyst.

But-2-ene produces butan-2-ol.

(i) Draw the structural formula for but-2-ene.

1

(ii) State why a catalyst is used in the reaction.

1

(b) Vinegar is made by dissolving ethanoic acid in water. The ethanoic acid is produced when ethanol is oxidised.

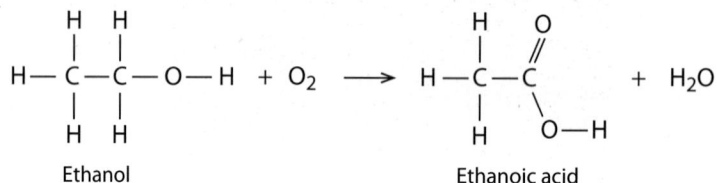

$$H-\overset{\overset{\displaystyle H}{|}}{\underset{\underset{\displaystyle H}{|}}{C}}-\overset{\overset{\displaystyle H}{|}}{\underset{\underset{\displaystyle H}{|}}{C}}-O-H \;+\; O_2 \;\longrightarrow\; H-\overset{\overset{\displaystyle H}{|}}{\underset{\underset{\displaystyle H}{|}}{C}}-\overset{\overset{\displaystyle O}{\diagup\!\diagup}}{\underset{\underset{\displaystyle O-H}{\diagdown}}{C}} \;+\; H_2O$$

Ethanol   Ethanoic acid

(i) Circle the functional group on ethanoic acid.

1

(ii) Vinegar is widely used as flavouring for food. Give another use of vinegar.

1

9. Liquid petroleum gas (LPG) is an alternative fuel to petrol.

Propane is the main gas in LPG. When propane burns it produces energy, carbon dioxide and water.

$$C_3H_8(g) + 5O_2(g) \longrightarrow 3CO_2(g) + 4H_2O(l)$$

(a) What name is given to a reaction where a substance reacts with oxygen to produce heat?

1

(b) LPG is also the fuel found in camping stoves.

A student used a camping stove to boil 2 litres of water. The starting temperature of the water was 23°C and the final temperature was 100°C.

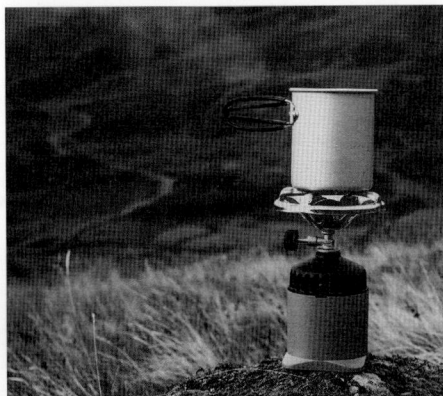

Calculate the energy released in kJ.

3

(c) Propane belongs to the alkane family. The energy released per mole of some alkanes is shown below.

Alkane	Energy kJmol l⁻¹ per mole
Propane	2202
Butane	2877
Pentane	3509
Hexane	4163
Heptane	4817
Octane	

(i) Predict the energy released per mole of octane. **1**

(ii) An advantage of LPG is that it produces less carbon dioxide per mole than octane, which is the main alkane in petrol.

Suggest a disadvantage of using LPG over petrol. **1**

10. Monster trucks use methanol as a fuel in place of petrol.

(a) To what family of compounds does methanol belong?

1

(b) Methanol is widely produced by reacting carbon monoxide with hydrogen in the presence of a catalyst.

$$CO(g) + 2H_2(g) \longrightarrow CH_3OH(l)$$

What mass of methanol would be produced by reacting 70 g of carbon monoxide completely with hydrogen?

3

11. A student set up the following cell.

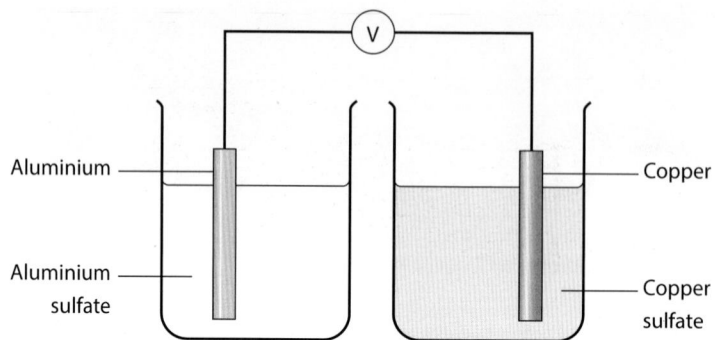

(a) What needs to be added to complete the cell?

1

(b) The following reactions occurred at the electrodes:

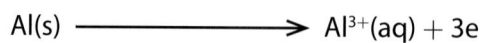

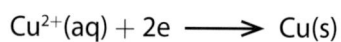

$$Al(s) \longrightarrow Al^{3+}(aq) + 3e$$

$$Cu^{2+}(aq) + 2e \longrightarrow Cu(s)$$

(i) Combine these to form a balanced redox equation.

1

(ii) Mark the path of electron flow on the diagram using arrows.

1

(iii) What effect would replacing copper with tin have on the voltage produced?

1

12. Aluminium is a metal commonly used to build aircraft.

(a) Explain why aluminium is more suitable for making aircraft than iron.

You may wish to use your data booklet to help you.

1

(b) Aluminium is the most abundant metal in the Earth's crust where it is commonly found in ores in the form of aluminium hydroxide and aluminium oxide.

The first time aluminium was extracted was in 1825, unlike copper which was extracted in prehistoric times.

Using your knowledge of chemistry, discuss why aluminium, which is more abundant than copper in the Earth's core, was only extracted from ores in recent history.

3

13. The main source of copper is its ore chalcopyrite ($CuFeS_2$). Rocks containing the ore are crushed and the ore is separated from the rock by a process called froth flotation. The concentrated ore is passed into the smelter where the copper is extracted. Sulfur dioxide is one of the waste products. The copper is not pure enough at this stage and has to undergo electrolytic refining to get it to 99·98 purity. Small quantities of gold, silver and platinum are recovered.

(a) Complete the flow diagram for the extraction and purification of copper.

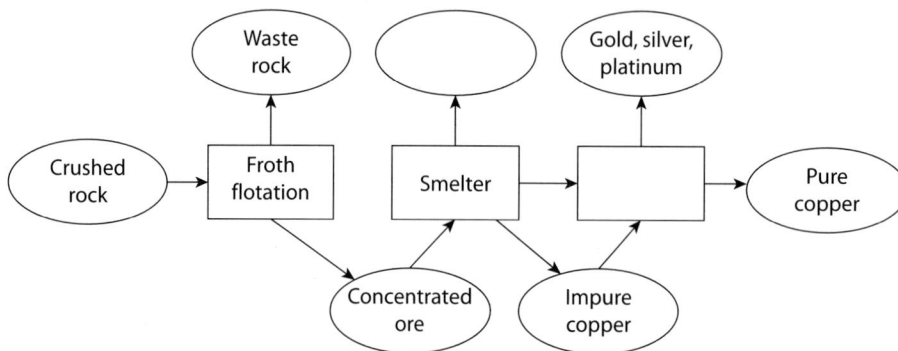

2

(b) Calculate the percentage by mass of copper in chalcopyrite ($CuFeS_2$).

Show your working clearly.

3

(c) Suggest why silver, gold and platinum are worth recovering during the process even though they only exist in small amounts.

1

(d) The diagram shows the copper purification step.

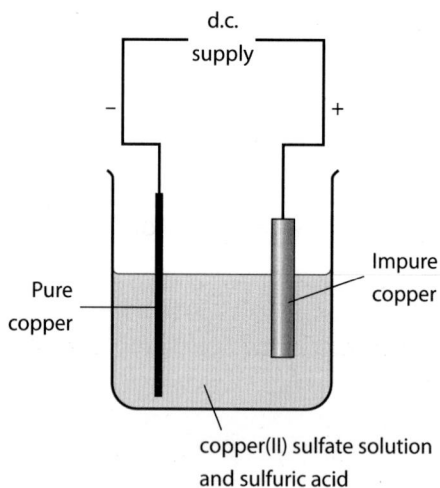

Write the ion-electron equation for the reaction taking place at the pure copper electrode.

You may wish to use your data booklet to help you.

1

14. Polyisobutene, a synthetic rubber, is a polymer which does not allow air through it. This makes it an important material in cling film, tyre inner tubes and the bladders in footballs.

A section containing three monomers of the polymer is shown below.

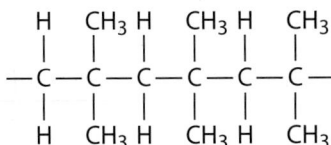

(a) Draw the monomer used to produce polyisobutene. **1**

(b) Write the systematic name for the monomer above. **1**

(c) What part of the monomer structure allows polymerisation to take place? **1**

(d) Butyl rubber is another synthetic rubber based on polyisobutene.

Butyl rubber contains two isobutene monomers joined to another monomer X.

A section of the polymer is shown below. Circle the part of the polymer structure due to monomer X in the structure below. **1**

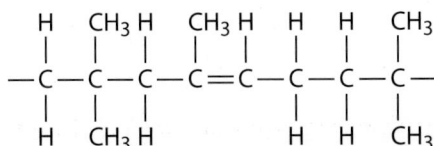

15. Smoke detectors in our homes contain a small amount of the radioisotope Americium 241.

Americium decays to form Neptunium 237.

The first stage in the decay series of Americium is:

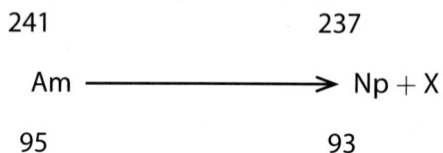

$$^{241}_{95}\text{Am} \longrightarrow \, ^{237}_{93}\text{Np} + \text{X}$$

(a) Name X.

1

(b) A 24 g sample of Americium took 916 years to decay to 6 g.

Calculate the half life of the sample.

2

16. Ammonia is an important starting material in the production of nitric acid, HNO_3.

Ammonia can be produced by the reaction between nitrogen and hydrogen.

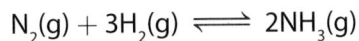

$$N_2(g) + 3H_2(g) \rightleftharpoons 2NH_3(g)$$

(a) What is meant by the $\rightleftharpoons$ in the above reaction?

1

(b) Oxides of nitrogen, NO_x, are needed to make nitric acid.

Oxides of nitrogen are produced by bubbling gas X through a solution of ammonium hydroxide.

These oxides can be produced in the laboratory using the apparatus below.

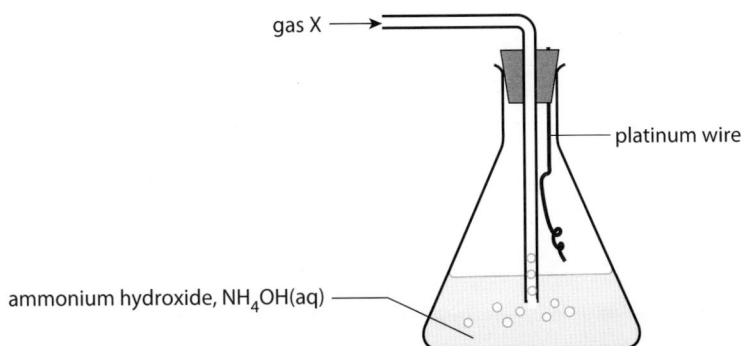

gas X

platinum wire

ammonium hydroxide, $NH_4OH(aq)$

(i) Name gas X.

1

(ii) The platinum wire is a catalyst and glows red hot as soon as the oxidation takes place.

What word can be used to describe this oxidation reaction?

1

(c) The reaction between nitric acid and ammonia produces an important fertiliser.

(i) Name this fertiliser.

1

(ii) Ammonium phosphate is another fertiliser.

Write the chemical formula for ammonium phosphate.

1